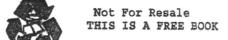

MOST WANTED

MOST WANTED

WANTED

A History of the
FBI's Ten Most Wanted List

MARK SABLJAK &
MARTIN H. GREENBERG

BONANZA BOOKS
New York

Copyright © 1990 by Mark Sabljak and Martin H. Greenberg

First published in 1990 by Bonanza Books, distributed by Outlet Book Company, Inc.,
a Random House Company, 225 Park Avenue South, New York, New York 10003

Printed and bound in the United States of America

Book design by Jean Krulis

Library of Congress Cataloging-in-Publication Data

Sabljak, Mark.
    Most wanted : a history of the FBI's ten most wanted list / Mark Sabljak & Martin H.
Greenberg.
        p.   cm.
    ISBN 0-517-69330-5
    1. Criminals—United States—Biography. 2. Fugitives from justice—United States—Biog-
raphy. I. Greenberg, Martin Harry.
II. Title.
HV6785.S17   1990   90-33200
                                                                          CIP

8 7 6 5 4 3 2 1

To Joan—

Here's to another fifteen years

Acknowledgments

Throughout the period of this book's research, members of the Federal Bureau of Investigation have proved extremely courteous and helpful to the authors. They have furnished the news releases, apprehension reports, photos, wanted posters, and other information on which the majority of this book's material was based.

In particular, we would like to thank Milt Ahlerich, Swanson Carter, Melanie McElhinney, Joyce Waters, and Silko Thomas of the FBI for their gracious help.

The material furnished by the Bureau, however, was always missing one key bit of information: the names of the special agents who labored long and hard to crack the cases and apprehend the Most Wanted fugitives. FBI policy forbids making them public. While this policy is understandable and justified, it may seem to those who read the book that only the Most Wanted fugitives were judged to be worth writing about. That is the furthest from the truth. In fact, the "unnamed heroes," the FBI's special agents and all law enforcement officials are the ones who truly made this book possible.

Contents

The History of the Ten Most Wanted List

The Federal Bureau of Investigation's Most Wanted program officially began on March 14, 1950, when FBI Director J. Edgar Hoover named Thomas J. Holden number one on the first Ten Most Wanted List. This new and rather dubious distinction brought to immediate public attention the convicted train robber and prison escapee sought for the 1949 murder of his wife and her two brothers at a Chicago drinking party. The rest of that famous Ten Most Wanted List included suspected safecrackers, prison escapees, murderers, and bank robbers.

Although J. Edgar Hoover, who had all but single-handedly developed the FBI into America's paramount crime-fighting organization, was well known for his love of positive publicity, the idea for the Ten Most Wanted List did not actually originate with the FBI. FBI history traces the idea to a story written by a reporter for the International News Service, which later became United Press International. In that story the reporter asked the Bureau for the names and descriptions of the "toughest guys" the FBI would like to capture. The popularity of the article undoubtedly was not lost on Hoover.

There is no doubt that the FBI's naming of a Public Enemy Number One during the gangster era of the 1930s and 1940s was the inspiration for the INS story. But many law enforcement officials saw a problem in naming just one individual to such a lofty "honor." Would not the warped minds of some criminals—wanting to claim the "Number One" title for their own—turn to even more violent crimes? And so the Ten Most Wanted List was devised.

How does the FBI pick its top ten? In a brief history of the List, the Bureau wrote:

> Special Agents from the Fugitive Unit of the Criminal Investigation Division, who are readily familiar with all current FBI fugitives, make the preliminary recommendation in conjunction with Special Agents from the Office of Congressional and Public Affairs, who coordinate fugitive publicity. In addition, many recommendations are received from the Bureau's 59 field offices. The selection is approved by the Assistant Director of the Criminal Investigative Division and the Assistant Director of the Public Affairs Sections, and finally by the Director.

What are the criteria for making the List? The Bureau said that there are two primary reasons. First, the fugitive must be considered a particularly dangerous menace to society and/or have a lengthy record of committing serious crimes. Second, the Bureau must believe nationwide publicity will assist in apprehending the fugitive.

The majority of the more than 400 fugitives who have made the Most Wanted List have been individuals who committed crimes in one area of the country and whose addition gives them their first national reputation.

There are exceptions. These include Joseph Corbett, Jr., wanted for questioning in the kidnaping and murder of millionaire brewer Adolph Coors III; James Earl Ray, who made the List twice, the first time after he was named the suspect in the assassination of Rev. Dr. Martin Luther King, Jr., and the second time after a short prison escape; and Angela Davis and other late 1960s and early 1970s radicals who gained fame even before they became Most Wanted fugitives.

The Most Wanted List has also included the widest variety of serious crimes—among them, mass murder, prison escape, kidnap, rape, bank robbery, and bombings.

While the Bureau is only allowed to search for "federal" fugitives, it can step in if someone wanted for a state crime is believed to have crossed state lines in their attempt to avoid capture. Then, a federal charge of "unlawful flight to avoid prosecution" filed against the fugitive makes them fair game for the FBI and a potential for the Most Wanted List.

The List hasn't always been limited to just ten. At least ten times during the course of FBI history, "special additions" have been named to the List, pushing its total at one time during the 1970s to sixteen. The first such "special addition" was assassination suspect James Earl Ray. The most recent was Alton Coleman, who was added in 1984 after leaving a trail of kidnaping and death through several Midwestern states.

Once a fugitive is named to the list, the Bureau prepares press releases for the nation's media, wanted posters for post offices, and cards for law enforcement agencies. These include photographs of the fugitive, fingerprints, and other details—such as a physical description, occupation, and hobbies—that might help lead to an apprehension.

The process is expensive. In 1983 the Bureau estimated that once an individual was placed on the list, the FBI would spend an estimated $20,000 to $30,000 to get the word out. At that time a fugitive's addition would be publicized by 900 news releases, 500 spot announcements for radio and television stations, 1,500 posters, and 1,000 photographs and placards for the 40,000 or so police departments around the country.

Once on the Most Wanted List, most fugitives' names are not removed until they meet one of three criteria: first, when they are captured, or in rare cases, found dead or thought to be dead; second, when the process against them is dismissed (not an FBI decision); third, when they no longer fit the conditions for the Top Ten.

There have been only four cases of removal. Three of the four were 1970s era revolutionaries. They were Dwight Armstrong and Leo Burt, both sought for the bombing of a University of Wisconsin facility in which a researcher was killed, and Katherine Power, wanted for several crimes, including her involvement with a bank robbery in which a Boston policeman was killed. While Armstrong was later captured, neither Burt nor Power have ever been arrested. The fourth fugitive removed from the List was Benjamin Paddock, a prison escapee, who was also arrested by FBI agents after his removal.

After their addition to the List, the fugitive becomes another entry in the FBI's numbers game. The Bureau's "averages" include:

- Average height of a fugitive: 5 feet 9 inches
- Average weight: 167 pounds
- Average age at time of apprehension: 36 years
- Average time on list: 157 days
- Average distance between crime scene and apprehension: 969 miles

The longest time anybody has been on the List continuously was eighteen years, four months, and nine days. This "honor" belongs to suspected cop killer Charles Lee Herron, who, on February 9, 1968, became the 265th fugitive added to the List. He was finally captured on June 18, 1986, just a few weeks short of the date that the Bureau named its 401st fugitive.

The shortest stay on the List was two hours. Billy Austin Bryant, who was later found guilty of murdering two FBI agents who were hunting for him, was added to the List at approximately 5:00 P.M. on January 8, 1969. He was captured at approximately 7:00 P.M. by members of the Washington, D.C., police.

Of the more than 400 fugitives added to the List before 1990, 398 have been apprehended, with tips from citizens figuring in at least 122 of the apprehensions. The majority of the arrests—well over 200—have been made by the FBI, with four surrenders, four suicides, just over 90 arrests by local authorities, and another 50 or so by joint federal and local forces.

FBI Director J. Edgar Hoover himself would congratulate any citizen who played a part in the apprehension in the early years, but he always did it privately, so as not to subject them to any retaliation by the fugitives or the fugitives' friends—a tradition that survives today.

While there is no doubt about the List's statistical success, the Most Wanted program has often been the target of critics. Early on, some cynics suggested that the Bureau often named to the List fugitives they were closing in on or those they knew would be arrested shortly.

In the 1970s the List fell under particularly heavy criticism. As attacks against Hoover and his programs reached new heights shortly before his death in 1972, the List was called a "political tool for suppression." Even an author who staunchly defended the program saw the expansion of the List to sixteen in the 1970s as diluting the impact.

But the List can and will survive. In the late 1980s, with a newly found source of publicity from the "America's Most Wanted" program on the Fox television network, fugitives again have had a chance to become nationally famous—a privilege often leading to their downfall.

So has the Most Wanted program been successful? Has it been worth the money? That is a difficult question to answer. The only reasonable response might be that if the Most Wanted List has led to just one arrest that prevented a serious crime or a murder, isn't that worth all the time, energy, and money put into it?

The next chapter takes a brief look at the history of the FBI and some of the infamous "Gangster Era" criminals—men such as John Dillinger and "Baby Face" Nelson—who helped make the Bureau's reputation before the Most Wanted List was instituted. Then, decade by decade, some of the most notorious Most Wanted fugitives are profiled. In addition to the main entries, each decade also presents a rogues' gallery of shorter entries and mug shots. Almost all of the photographs provided by the FBI show some retouching; these have been reproduced here just as they appear in the FBI's files.

While this book is meant to chronicle many of the cases that have made up the fabled history of the Most Wanted program, it is by no means complete. Some of the FBI's own files are missing key details; others lack apprehension reports, conviction follow-ups, or photographs. Nor can this book be totally objective. Based for the most part on the FBI's own records, it by nature lacks material that is critical of the Bureau.

Before
the
Ten Most Wanted
List

To most Americans, the history of the FBI is contained in a single name—that of its famous director J. Edgar Hoover. Hoover directed ("ruled over" might be more accurate) the Bureau for decades; his beliefs and personal quirks were seemingly unquestioned, even by presidents and Congress.

While Hoover certainly played the central role in the Bureau's rise in size and stature, the FBI had actually been founded years earlier. The Bureau's main function is to be the investigative service of the Department of Justice, with the director reporting to the attorney general of the United States.

Before the Bureau was founded, the attorney general was forced to use US marshals and regional attorneys to investigate and apprehend offenders. At times, Federal Bank examiners, agents for the Customs Bureau, the Interior Department, and the Secret Service—even Pinkerton detectives—were drafted by the attorney general.

In 1908 President Theodore Roosevelt directed the attorney general to set up an investigative service within the Department of Justice, and a year later the agency was given a title—the Bureau of Investigation.

One of the Bureau's first targets were violators of the White Slave Traffic Act, otherwise known as the Mann Act, which forbids interstate transportation of women for prostitution. A famous victim of the act was heavyweight boxing champion Jack Johnson, who ended up in jail as a result of a trip with his fiancée, a former prostitute.

In the years before and during World War I, the Bureau of Investigation was assigned to track down draft "slacks" and Communist party members. Clearly, however, the Bureau was undermanned, politically controlled, and hardly ready for such challenges as the Black Tom Explosion of 1916, in which a blast of 2 million pounds of dynamite destroyed a shipping transfer point for the war effort in New York Harbor.

Three years later, another bomb blast helped give rise to the career of a young employee of the Bureau. On the evening of June 2, 1919, a bomb went off on the first floor of the residence of the newly appointed attorney general, A. Mitchell Palmer. The blast blew in the front of the house, shattered the library, cracked the ceiling, broke windows, and knocked pictures from the wall. The front windows of another house on the street, belonging to Assistant Secretary of the Navy Franklin D. Roosevelt, were blown out. Two men—thought to be the saboteurs—died in the blast; parts of their bodies were scattered throughout the neighborhood.

Other prominent politicians, judges, and businessmen were targeted with similar blasts, and Palmer decided to create a special General Intelligence Division within the Bureau to study subversive activities in the United States—to determine their scope and what action could be taken in the field of prosecution. Heading the division was twenty-four-year-old J. Edgar Hoover, then a special assistant to the attorney general.

Hoover's work led to what has become known as "Palmer's Red Raids," in which Communist leaders were seized and deported under existing US laws.

Though Hoover's star had risen, it was politics that gave him his ultimate opportunity when the Bureau was rocked with scandal in the early 1920s. It came to light that agents had been directed to routinely break into offices, read personal files, and keep information on the private lives of members of Congress who were then demanding investigations of reported corruption —including the Teapot Dome scandal—in the administration of President Warren G. Harding.

Testimony in front of Congress on the situation within the Department of Justice, including the Bureau of Investigation, led one historian to say the department had "reached its lowest ebb in morale, morals and efficiency." In 1924 President Calvin Coolidge demanded the resignation of Attorney General Harry Daugherty, and Harlan Fiske Stone, former dean of the Columbia University School of Law, was named attorney general.

A little over a month later, William J. Burns resigned as director of the Bureau, and from within, J. Edgar Hoover, then twenty-nine, was tapped as acting director. In the Bureau's own history, written by Don Whitehead, the scene is described this way:

"Hoover took a seat. Stone peered at him over his glasses and the two men looked at each other across the desk. Then Stone said abruptly, 'Young man, I want you to be the Acting Director of the Bureau of Investigation.'

"Hoover said, 'I'll take the job, Mr. Stone, on certain conditions.'

" 'What are they?'

" 'The Bureau must be divorced from politics and not be a catchall for political hacks. Appointments must be based on merit. Second, promotions will be made on proved ability and the Bureau will be responsible only to the Attorney General.' "

Whitehead wrote that Stone scowled and said, "I wouldn't give it to you under any other conditions. That's all. Good day."

Seven months later, Hoover became the director. But it took years to rid the Bureau of the abuses of previous decades. Stone went on to become a Supreme Court justice. But he watched over the Bureau and, on January 2, 1932, wrote Hoover: "I often look back to the days when I first made your acquaintance in the Department of Justice and it is always a comfort to me to see how completely you have confirmed my judgment when I decided to place you at the head of the Bureau of Investigation. The Government can now take pride in the Bureau instead of feeling obliged to apologize for it."

But Hoover wasn't satisfied with just cleaning house at the Bureau. He began a campaign that was to endure for many more decades, during which he would see the Bureau rise to the front ranks of the government's fight against crime.

The FBI's real impact on the public came in the Gangster Era of the 1930s and 1940s, when the Bureau was given the right and muscle to go after the criminal element that was running rampant throughout the country. One such brazen example was the Kansas City Massacre of June 17, 1933. On that date Frank Nash—an escaped convict who had been arrested in Hot Springs, Arkansas, by FBI agents and the police chief of McAlester, Oklahoma—was to arrive at the Union Railway Station in Kansas City, Missouri, on his way to the federal penitentiary at Leavenworth.

Awaiting the lawmen were three other FBI agents and two Kansas City detectives. Also waiting, however, were Vern Miller, a member of the Keating-Holden-Nash gang, with some recruited friends, among them Adam Richetti and Charles "Pretty Boy" Floyd.

The gunmen confronted the lawmen with machine guns and opened fire. The two detectives, the police chief, and one FBI agent were killed, and two other men were wounded. Nash was also killed, with a bullet in the brain, but all the attackers were able to escape.

In the search that followed, Miller's body was found, riddled with bullets, on the outskirts of Detroit on November 29, 1933. Richetti was captured on October 20, 1934, and executed in the gas chamber in Missouri four years later. Floyd was traced to a farm in Ohio, where he shot it out with FBI agents and local police. He was killed in a blaze of gunfire.

Another big-name capture also led to the FBI's first popular nickname—G-men. The Bureau was called in to investigate the kidnaping of a businessman from Oklahoma City, Oklahoma, who had been blindfolded and taken on a long automobile ride. He was eventually released after a $200,000 ransom was paid. But by giving the FBI key clues from his time as a captive, he was able to lead the Bureau to a ranch home near Paradise, Texas.

There the Bureau began to follow a path that led them to Memphis, Tennessee, and George "Machine Gun" Kelly. Traced to his hideaway, Kelly was caught without a machine gun in his hands, and when faced with drawn guns, he pleaded, "Don't shoot, G-men! Don't shoot, G-men!"

In 1934, Congress helped the FBI become even more effective by passing legislation that allowed the Bureau to enter into types of cases from which it had been excluded in the past. Now it became a federal crime to assault or kill a federal officer, to rob a federal bank, and to flee across state lines to avoid prosecution. FBI agents, who had been able to carry guns only in certain circumstances, were given full arrest powers and permission to be armed in carrying out their duties. It was laws such as these that allowed the FBI to join the chase for John Dillinger, probably the most notorious of the Gangster Era bad men.

Dillinger's reign of terror began in 1933, when he was paroled from the Indiana State Penitentiary after already having served eight and a half years of a sentence for assault and battery with intent to rob, and conspiracy to commit a felony. Dillinger's fellow townspeople signed a petition to have him released.

Only weeks later, Dillinger and two accomplices robbed a bank in New Carlisle, Indiana, of $10,600. Then—in each of the next three months— they robbed one more Indiana bank. Later that year, Dillinger engineered a prison break for ten bank robbers in Michigan City, Indiana. Dillinger was then arrested, but he escaped and went back to the business of robbing banks.

Dillinger was arrested again early in 1934 in Tucson, Arizona, while "vacationing" but was returned to Ohio to face charges. On March 3, 1934, Dillinger used a "gun" carved from wood to force a guard to release him. He then committed the error that brought the FBI into the case: he stole the sheriff's automobile and headed into Illinois. In crossing the state line, Dillinger had broken his first federal law, and the FBI was now on the case.

On April 22 the Bureau closed in on Dillinger and his gang at the Little Bohemia Lodge at Manitowish Waters, Wisconsin, but despite their having surrounded him, the gangster escaped after a gunfight. Three months later, Dillinger wasn't so lucky. On July 22, 1934, he walked out of Chicago's Biograph Theater with the "Woman in Red," who had set him up. Dillinger was approached by Melvin Purvis and other agents. He reached for a gun in his pocket but did not make it. Five shots hit him and he fell to the pavement, dying.

One of the key agents involved in the Dillinger arrest, Samuel Cowley, was killed that November in a gunfight with "Baby Face" Nelson. The battle claimed another FBI agent and Nelson.

The Bureau nabbed several other famous gangsters before the end of the decade. In 1935 the Bureau closed in on and killed Fred Barker and Ma Barker in Lake Weir, Florida. In 1936, Hoover himself—criticized by a senator for never having made an arrest—flew to New Orleans, where he and a squad of agents apprehended Alvin "Old Creepy" Karpis, a former associate of the Barkers who was involved in several kidnapings, burglaries, and murders. These arrests led to a wave of publicity, in film and in magazine and newspaper stories. Atop it all, J. Edgar Hoover was crowned the number one G-man.

FBI Headquarters

J. Edgar Hoover

GEORGE R. KELLY

ALIAS "MACHINE GUN KELLY"

- KIDNAPER.

- PARTICIPATED IN URSCHEL KID-NAPING ON JULY 22, 1933.

- APPREHENDED ON SEPTEMBER 26, 1933, IN MEMPHIS, TENNESSEE, BY FBI AGENTS.

- FIRST CRIMINAL TO CALL FBI AGENTS "G-MEN".

- CONVICTED AND SENTENCED TO LIFE IMPRISONMENT.

- DIED IN PENITENTIARY IN 1954.

Bonnie Parker

Clyde Barrow

IDENTIFICATION ORDER NO. 1217
March 12, 1934.

DIVISION OF INVESTIGATION
U. S. DEPARTMENT OF JUSTICE
WASHINGTON, D. C.

Fingerprint Classification

```
12  9 R O
.14 U 00 9
```

WANTED

JOHN DILLINGER, with alias,

FRANK SULLIVAN

NATIONAL MOTOR VEHICLE THEFT ACT

DESCRIPTION

Age, 31 years
Height, 5 feet 7-1/8 inches
Weight, 153 pounds
Build, medium
Hair, medium chestnut
Eyes, grey
Complexion, medium
Occupation, machinist
Marks and scars, 1/2 inch scar
  back left hand; scar middle
  upper lip; brown mole between
  eyebrows
Mustache

Photograph taken January 25, 1934

CRIMINAL RECORD

As John Dillinger, #14395, received State Reformatory, Pendleton, Indiana, September 16, 1924; crime, assault and battery with intent to rob and conspiracy to commit a felony; sentences, 2 to 14 years and 10 to 20 years respectively;

As John Dillinger, #13225, received State Prison, Michigan City, Indiana, July 16, 1929; transferred from Indiana State Reformatory; paroled under Reformatory jurisdiction, May 10, 1933; parole revoked by Governor - considered as delinquent parolee;

As John Dillinger, #10587, arrested Police Department, Dayton, Ohio, September 22, 1933; charge, fugitive; turned over to Allen County, Ohio, authorities;

As John Dillinger, received County Jail, Lima, Ohio, September 28, 1933; charge, bank robbery; escaped October 12, 1933;

As Frank Sullivan, arrested Police Department, Tucson, Arizona, January 25, 1934; charge, fugitive; turned over to Lake County, Indiana, authorities;

As John Dillinger, #14487, arrested Sheriff's Office, Crown Point, Indiana, January 30, 1934; charge, murder - bank robbery; escaped March 3, 1934.

The United States Marshal, Chicago, Illinois, holds warrant of arrest charging John Dillinger with feloniously and knowingly transporting Ford V-8 four door sedan, motor number 256447, property of Lillian Holley, Sheriff, Lake County, Indiana, from Crown Point, Indiana to Chicago, Illinois, on or about March 3, 1934.

Law enforcement agencies kindly transmit any additional information or criminal record to the nearest office of the Division of Investigation, U. S. Department of Justice.

If apprehended, please notify the Director, Division of Investigation, U. S. Department of Justice, Washington, D. C., or the Special Agent in Charge of the Office of the Division of Investigation listed on the back hereof which is nearest your city.

(over)   Issued by: J. EDGAR HOOVER, DIRECTOR.

John Dillinger

Al Capone

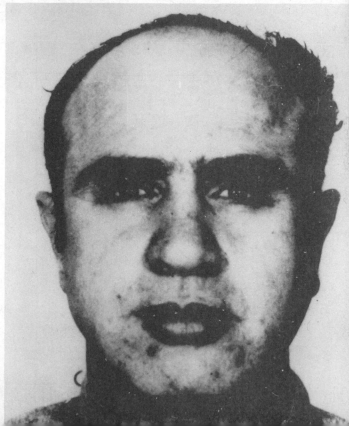

ALVIN KARPIS

- MEMBER OF BARKER-KARPIS GANG.

- CRIMINAL CAREER DATED FROM 1926. INCLUDED ARRESTS FOR BURGLARY, AUTO THEFT AND KIDNAPING.

- PARTICIPATED IN BREMER AND OTHER KIDNAPINGS.

- APPREHENDED BY DIRECTOR HOOVER AND FBI AGENTS ON MAY 1, 1936, IN NEW ORLEANS, LOUISIANA.

ADAM RICHETTI

- ASSOCIATE OF "PRETTY BOY" FLOYD.

- MEMBER OF BARKER-KARPIS GANG.

- CRIMINAL RECORD INCLUDES ARRESTS FOR ROBBERY AND MURDER.

- PARTICIPATED IN KANSAS CITY MASSACRE, JUNE 17, 1933.

- CAPTURED OCTOBER 20, 1934, TRIED IN MARCH, 1935, AND EXECUTED IN GAS CHAMBER ON OCTOBER 7, 1938.

"BABY FACE NELSON"
ALIAS OF LESTER J. GILLIS

- MEMBER OF DILLINGER GANG.

- KILLER AND BANK ROBBER IN MIDWEST.

- DURING HIS CRIMINAL CAREER NELSON KILLED 3 FBI AGENTS.

- NELSON WAS KILLED IN A GUN BATTLE WITH FBI AGENTS ON NOVEMBER 27, 1934, AT BARRINGTON, ILLINOIS.

VERNON C. MILLER
ALIAS "VERN" MILLER

- MEMBER OF KEATING-HOLDEN-NASH GANG.

- GUNMAN, KILLER AND GANGSTER.

- PARTICIPATED IN KANSAS CITY MASSACRE, JUNE 17, 1933.

- HE WAS FOUND DEAD IN THE ENVIRONS OF DETROIT, MICHIGAN, NOVEMBER 29, 1933.

The 1950s

Introduction

The first Most Wanted List actually took the FBI only eleven days to compile. J. Edgar Hoover's own Bureau—never one to settle for a single newspaper story when ten might be possible—released one Most Wanted fugitive a day from May 14, 1950, when "Tough Tommy" Holden was given the first number one position, through May 24, when Morris Guralnick, who had once bitten off a policeman's finger, was added on as number ten.

In a matter of only days, the Most Wanted List paid its first dividend: William Nesbit, the number three fugitive, was recognized by six youths from St. Paul, Minnesota, who had seen his photograph in a local newspaper story.

While the Most Wanted List met with much early success, it also had some failures. Frederick Tenuto, a murderer and prison escapee, was added to the List as number fourteen on May 24, 1950. His name was finally removed from the List on March 9, 1964, with the Bureau reporting that Tenuto was rumored to be dead.

Tenuto was typical of the criminals who made the Most Wanted List in the 1950s—a hodgepodge of prison escapees, bank robbers, burglars, and car thieves.

No. 1
THOMAS J. HOLDEN

First Most Wanted Listing:
March 14, 1950
Apprehended:
June 23, 1951

The first man on the Most Wanted List certainly lived up to his official billing. Train robber, prison escapee, and wife murderer, "Tough Tommy" Holden provoked the FBI into writing one of its most flowery press releases. Fittingly, the first man on the Most Wanted List was brought down by his new public notoriety.

The FBI wrote: "Crime we have had with us always. We will continue to have crime so long as man's basic passions and instincts survive. Crime can, however, be minimized.

"The devastating effects of crime are to some extent reduced by quick apprehension of those engaged in criminal activity. Thomas James Holden is one man whose freedom in society is a menace to every man, woman and child in America."

Holden earned his reputation over three lawless decades. He began his criminal career in the 1920s and was tagged as one of the most notorious train robbers since Jesse James. Convicted for robbing a mail train in the late 1920s, he was sent to the federal prison at Leavenworth, Kansas, but he made what the FBI called an "ingenious" escape and renewed contacts with "such notorious mobsters as Alvin Karpis, Vern Miller and Frank Nash."

Not content to enjoy his freedom quietly, he was said to have been one of the outside crew members responsible for the sensational armed break from Leavenworth in December 1931.

With the FBI on his trail again, his two-year break ended, the FBI said, "on July 7, 1932 when Special Agents and local officers surrounded him and a fellow escapee on a golf course at Kansas City, Mo. The pair was armed only with their golf clubs."

Holden was imprisoned again, this time until 1947. But times had changed. Many of his criminal friends were no longer around. The FBI said, "A number of the more reckless desperadoes elected to 'shoot it out' with law enforcement officers and died in the attempt to escape. Others, luckier —or smarter—were in Alcatraz or similar institutions of government hospitality."

Holden made sure his freedom was short-lived when on June 5, 1949, police found the bodies of a woman and two men in a Chicago apartment. The victims were Mrs. Lillian Holden, his wife, and her two brothers. Police said Holden had shot them with a .38 revolver after a drinking party.

After he was seen in Indiana, the FBI was called in to aid in the search. Holden was finally captured thousands of miles away in Beaverton, Oregon, where he was working as a plasterer. The FBI said that a fellow worker had recognized a picture of Holden run in the *Portland Oregonian* and tipped them off.

No. 2
MORLEY V. KING

First Most Wanted Listing:
March 15, 1950
Apprehended:
October 31, 1951

Morley King was opening oysters in a Philadelphia restaurant when FBI agents confronted him. "I wondered when the FBI would get me," he was quoted as having remarked.

King, of Wheeling, West Virginia, was wanted for the murder of his wife in San Luis Obispo, California, on July 1, 1947.

Agents said that the four-year search for King ended when they found him working as second chef in the restaurant.

No. 3
WILLIAM R. NESBIT

First Most Wanted Listing:
March 16, 1950
Apprehended:
March 18, 1950

William Nesbit, a fifty-year-old convicted murderer, met his match in a group of teenage boys from St. Paul, Minnesota.

The youths saw Nesbit's picture in a local newspaper and recognized him as a "hermit" they had seen living in a cave. Wanting to make sure he was the man, the boys—armed with only an "atomic ray gun," Boy Scout knives, and sling shots—jammed snow down the cave's exposed stovepipe. Sure enough, Nesbit was smoked out. The boys confirmed their suspicions and then ran to police, who made the actual capture.

With Nesbit's apprehension on March 18, 1950, the FBI pulled in the first fugitive since the Most Wanted List had been released, and a convict involved with one of the more sensational crimes of that time was brought to justice.

On New Year's Eve, 1936, ex-convict Floyd Parker and his girlfriend, Helen Sieler, had been shot and left for dead in the powderhouse of a WPA project, just before seven tons of dynamite and black powder exploded. The blast shattered plate glass worth $20,000 in the downtown district of Sioux Falls, South Dakota, almost five miles away, and caused a near panic among New Year's Eve revelers. The noise of the explosion was heard as far as fifty miles away.

Fingered in the crime were Lee Bradley, Harry "Slim" Reeves, and Nesbit, all members of a gang involved in a $37,000 jewel robbery at Sioux City, Iowa. Police said that the shooting was a result of an argument between Bradley and Parker. Bradley said that the gang was attempting to break into the powderhouse to obtain dynamite when Bradley made a "disparaging" remark about Sieler.

Bradley said that Parker attacked him first with his fist, then with a hammer, but that he was able to draw a gun. He described the scene: "I shot. He fell like a dog. I rolled him over and he was dead. I had shot him in the heart."

Bradley also mentioned that Reeves then asked what they would do with the woman, fearing she would "squawk." He said, "She knelt over Parker, and as she did, Reeves grabbed the hammer and began hitting her over the head. She keeled over. Then when she cried to Billy [Nesbit] for help, Reeves shot her.

"I guess we must have all thought of the same thing at the same time, 'Let's get rid of those bodies,' so we picked them up and tossed them into the powderhouse. I thought Miss Sieler was dead, too, because she didn't make a sound.

"We all helped toss the bodies in, but I won't say who lit the fuse. Then we ran to the car and were five to six miles away when the explosion came."

All three men were later captured. Nesbit was sentenced to a life term, later commuted to twenty years, but even that was not soon enough for him. In 1946 Nesbit escaped from the South Dakota State Penitentiary.

Four years later the FBI added him to the Most Wanted List, and Nesbit stayed on the run. His last accommodations were hardly posh. For four months Nesbit lived in a cave formerly used by a brewery, on the Mississippi River near St. Paul, Minnesota. The cave had a wooden floor plus a cot, stove, and cupboard. Police said Nesbit had plenty of food and a pail of fresh water from a nearby spring.

He was not able to keep entirely out of the public eye. A group of neighborhood youngsters befriended and visited him because they thought he was "just a bum who didn't have much." The boys even gave him a hatchet and canteen, which were later found in the cave by the authorities.

But one of the boys began to suspect Nesbit's identity after spotting a picture of him in a newspaper "wanted" column. The next day, the gang went to the cave and smoked him out. When the police arrived, Nesbit surrendered without a struggle. The boys became heroes. J. Edgar Hoover sent a congratulatory message—a practice he continued with every citizen who cooperated on an arrest—and an invitation to visit him sometime. Two of the boys flew to Washington, D.C., to meet the FBI director. They were accompanied by a feature writer from the *St. Paul Dispatch,* which financed the trip. The boys' trip to Washington also included a tour of the Capitol Building and other attractions.

Newspaper stories around the country quoted the boys liberally. One story went on to say that neither boy would say whether "they were packing firearms" as they boarded the plane. "We ain't saying anything about that," one boy said, mysteriously giving a significant hoist to his belt. And about the dramatic capture he said, "Naw, I wasn't scared. We could have handled him."

Nesbit, meanwhile, was found guilty of escape, and served an additional three years in prison before he was paroled in 1954.

No. 4
HENRY R. MITCHELL

First Most Wanted Listing:
March 17, 1950
Process Dismissed:
July 18, 1958

The last member of the original Most Wanted List was dropped from it on July 18, 1958. The FBI's search for Henry Mitchell—sought on bank robbery charges—ended when charges against him were dismissed.

Mitchell had been sought following a $10,353 armed robbery of a Florida bank on January 21, 1948. While his partner was caught later, Mitchell himself remained free, despite the significant amounts of publicity generated when the list was first announced and also by the frequent follow-up stories.

According to sources, Mitchell might have been eliminated by other criminals. And so in 1958, when he was sixty-three years old, all charges against him were dismissed.

No. 5
OMAR A. PINSON

First Most Wanted Listing:
March 18, 1950
Apprehended:
August 28, 1950

Omar Pinson had one of the strangest hideaways of any Most Wanted fugitive—he was buried in a grave.

Pinson led what could be conservatively called a life of crime. He was sentenced to eighteen months in prison in Iowa in 1936 on a charge of armed robbery. After his release he spent time in the Missouri prison system (beginning in 1941) for automobile tampering and in the Washington system (beginning in 1944) for burglary.

Pinson resumed his criminal trade—home burglary—and specialized in obtaining firearms, which he could fence easily.

On April 25, 1947, in Hood River, Oregon, Pinson was returning to his truck after a burglary, armed with a .32-20 automatic, when he was confronted by an Oregon State police officer. Pinson killed him, then eluded capture by running a blockade and riding a freight train, only to be finally apprehended in Ordnance, Oregon, the next day.

Sentenced to the Oregon State Penitentiary, he took part in two botched attempts at escape. In one, convicts held a knife to a guard's neck and tried to drive a truck across a railroad bridge leading out of the prison, and in the other, a fire was set in a prison flax mill for a diversion.

On May 30, 1949, Pinson finally made good on his getaway, sawing his way out of his own cell and crawling through an eight- by twelve-inch opening. He then released a fellow convict and sawed through the bars of the cell block before fleeing the prison grounds amid a hail of gunfire.

Pinson's partner in the scheme was later arrested in Columbus, Ohio. He claimed that Pinson had died of gunshot wounds suffered during the escape attempt and that he had buried Pinson a few miles east of Kellogg, Idaho.

While police attempted to locate Pinson's grave, an individual with the name Joseph Dorian became the object of a widespread search in Washington and Idaho on charges of burglary. Within one day, Dorian was arrested twice by officers in northern Idaho, yet he escaped each time. After Dorian eluded officers, his automobile was searched and found to contain three revolvers, a rifle, ammunition, a gas mask, and a case of burglary tools. It was also determined that Dorian was Omar Pinson.

Pinson was finally located in 1950 when a man resembling him purchased a 1942 Ford Dakota. With officers on alert, Pinson was stopped in Pierre, South Dakota, by an officer of the highway patrol and an FBI National Academy graduate assigned to the South Dakota Attorney General's Office. Even then, Pinson was able to escape by using the back door of the police department, but he was chased two blocks and caught.

After his capture, Pinson told a story of having been buried alive in Idaho by the man with whom he had escaped from prison. Pinson was alleged to have stated: "I went out of my head from a fever. . . . The man told me I was going to die and asked me what he should do. I remember telling him to bury me." Pinson said that he awoke to find himself in a ditch covered with rocks and sticks. "I don't know how long I laid there," he said.

After his capture, Pinson was said to have muttered, "This living on the run is no good. You come into town and find your picture on the post office wall, and so you light out again. You've got to be careful of everybody you meet."

No. 6
LEE EMORY DOWNS

First Most Wanted Listing:
March 20, 1950
Apprehended:
April 7, 1950

Lee Downs kept "bad" company. A forty-three-year-old native of Butte, Montana, he was known as an expert safecracker who had operated with holdup men and burglars in three Pacific states.

He joined the List after a $10,800 holdup of a telephone company office in San Jose, California, but was arrested across the nation in Daytona Beach, Florida. Downs was the third Most Wanted fugitive arrested since the Most Wanted List's release.

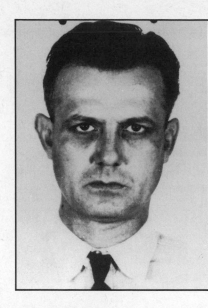

No. 7
ORBA ELMER JACKSON

First Most Wanted Listing:
March 21, 1950
Apprehended:
March 22, 1950

Orba Jackson walked away from an "honor farm" on March 23, 1947, while serving a twenty-five-year sentence for robbing a US post office. But he could not hide from the publicity of the FBI's Most Wanted List.

After fleeing from the federal penitentiary in Platte County, Missouri, Jackson signed on as a farm hand in Oregon. But the first List's publicity drew the attention of a local resident, who saw Jackson's picture on the wall of an Oregon post office, then confirmed his suspicions when he read a story and saw a photograph of Jackson in a local paper.

FBI agents and local police arrested Jackson without incident.

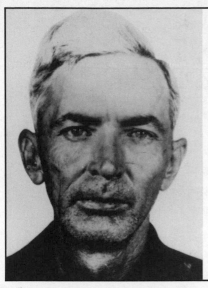

No. 8
GLEN ROY WRIGHT

First Most Wanted Listing:
March 22, 1950
Apprehended:
June 23, 1950

The FBI relies not only on citizens to help in their effort to capture wanted criminals, but on informants as well. Such was the case of Glen Roy Wright, an escapee fleeing from the Oklahoma State Penitentiary.

Wright, who was jailed in 1934 for armed robbery, escaped from prison in 1948. His freedom lasted only a few months after the first Most Wanted List was released.

On December 13, 1950, Wright was apprehended in a Salina, Kansas, drugstore. FBI records show that an informant helped them capture Wright.

The informant's name was never released, and FBI files show great pains taken to protect the source, including the use of various aliases in official correspondence.

No. 9
HENRY HARLAND SHELTON

First Most Wanted Listing:
March 23, 1950
Apprehended:
June 23, 1950

The newspaper headline read "FBI Guns Stop Henry Shelton" and "One of 10 Most Wanted Criminals Reaches for Automatic Too Late."

Henry Shelton was involved in one of the most violent arrests of the original Most Wanted lineup when, on June 23, 1950, he attempted to shoot it out with FBI agents who approached him in front of an Indianapolis tavern.

Imprisoned in upper Michigan for bank robbery, Shelton escaped in the fall of 1949. He commandeered a car and, holding the driver hostage with a knife, forced him to drive through Wisconsin and Illinois before the man escaped in Montmorenci, Indiana.

Two FBI agents confronted Shelton outside a tavern. The bar owner said that she heard an agent say, "Come on, fella, it's all over."

"That's what you think," Shelton replied, reaching for an automatic stuck in his belt. Both agents fired, and Shelton collapsed on the sidewalk before he could shoot. Despite two bullet wounds, Shelton was able to drink a bottle of beer and smoke a cigarette before the ambulance arrived.

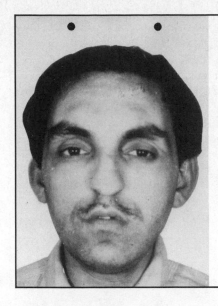

No. 10
MORRIS GURALNICK

First Most Wanted Listing:
March 24, 1950
Apprehended:
December 15, 1950

Morris Guralnick was not a nice man. So the FBI made no attempt to hide its fervor to catch Guralnick, who had stabbed his former girlfriend and bitten off the finger of a police officer.

In its press release, the FBI said of Guralnick:

> A product of the slums of New York City's east side, Morris Guralnick is high on the list of most wanted men. He has earned the spot. Highly emotional and violent, his vicious and apparently uncontrollable actions have marked him as an extremely dangerous fugitive. . . .
>
> . . . In view of his emotional instability and previous vicious acts—he has been characterized as "a wild-eyed" person—this fugitive is a constant menace to society.
>
> Guralnick is extremely short—approximately five feet, four inches in height—and weighs approximately 138 pounds. His appearance is distinctive because of his size and because of a broken nose (bridge), two upper front teeth missing and his sloping forehead.

Guralnick was said to be a constant frequenter of burlesque theaters; his only known jobs were in carnivals as a popcorn vendor or candy butcher.

In April 1948 Guralnick allegedly stabbed his former girlfriend and then, while being taken into custody, resisted violently and bit off the finger of an arresting police officer.

While awaiting trial in Kingston, New York, Guralnick and four other inmates broke the jail's plumbing fixtures and brutally assaulted two jail guards with broken pipes while making their escape.

Months later, a Madison, Wisconsin, resident was paging through a copy of *Coronet* magazine. He saw a picture of a wanted fugitive whom he recognized as "Ben Glass," a former employee of a Madison luggage store.

The citizen contacted the Madison Police Department, which called in the FBI. This combined effort found Guralnick living in a rented apartment and working at a local clothing store. When confronted, Guralnick attempted to flee, but he was overpowered.

No. 11
WILLIAM F. SUTTON

First Most Wanted Listing:
March 20, 1950
Apprehended:
February 18, 1952

Willie Sutton was not the richest bank robber in US history, but he was certainly one of the most colorful robbers of his era.

Sutton, nicknamed Willie the Actor, was born on the Brooklyn waterfront in 1901 and had become a burglar by the age of ten. At seventeen he was in jail, and in 1926, at the age of twenty-five, he made his first trip to "escape-proof" Sing Sing.

By the time Sutton's career finally ended in 1952, he had robbed banks of more than $2 million and escaped from prison twice—including one getaway from Sing Sing.

Sutton's trademark was his disguises. In 1929, while walking down Broadway, he got an idea when he saw armored truck guards being waved into a building merely by their uniforms. "That afternoon, Willie the Actor was born," Sutton later recalled. Wearing the disguise of a Western Union messenger, he made his first big score, netting some $130,000 in gems from a Brooklyn jewelry store.

A police inspector, sent to investigate the robbery of a Brooklyn bank Sutton had subsequently taken for $48,000, was heard to say, "Looks like Willie the Actor has been here."

"Why did I rob banks?" Sutton later mused. "Because I enjoyed it. I loved it. I was more alive when I was inside a bank, robbing it, than at any other time in my life."

The eleventh Most Wanted fugitive, Sutton joined the List after prison escapes in 1932 and in 1947.

While he may have had thousands of dollars in loot stashed away, it was his frugality that finally cost him his freedom. Sutton tried to save himself a $1.50 charge for servicing his car. Instead of letting a garage mechanic drive a block to change a run-down battery, he chose to wait a few hours and lug the battery to the car himself. He was just about to start toward his car when the police moved in. Sutton had $7,000 in his pockets and $2,000 more in his room when arrested.

Sutton's arrest came following a tip from a twenty-four-year-old Broadway pants salesman. Tragically, the tipster, Arnold Schuster, who had spotted Sutton in a subway and trailed him until he found a policeman, was murdered less than a month after Sutton's arrest. The revenge killer pumped four bullets into his head and two more into his stomach when Schuster was just ten doors from his home.

No. 13
HENRY CLAY TOLLETT

First Most Wanted Listing:
April 11, 1950
Apprehended:
June 3, 1950

Henry Tollett was arrested twice by FBI agents. He didn't live long enough to try for a third time.

In 1947 Tollett was part of a four-man gang that robbed banks along the West Coast of tens of thousands of dollars. But authorities caught up with the gang, and the FBI arrested Tollett and his companions later that year.

Upon his arrest, $1,060 was located in the steering post of Tollett's car. Several months later, he admitted his participation in the crimes and led FBI agents to a cache near Bakersfield, California, where he had buried $13,000.

Tollett was sentenced to serve twenty-five years in prison and was sent to the US Penitentiary at McNeil Island, Washington. On November 22, 1949, the warden at the prison reported to the FBI that Tollett was discovered missing during the noon count when the cannery crew reported for their meal. An investigation led to the belief that Tollett had concealed himself in a load of newly refinished furniture that had left the prison by ferry shortly before he was missed. Tollett had had easy access to the truck during loading.

On June 4, 1951, the FBI's San Francisco office was contacted by the California Highway Patrol, which reported that they had taken into custody an individual identified as Lewis Basham, who had been driving what they believed was a stolen automobile.

The arresting officer stated that during the arrest Basham had been shot and critically wounded and had been taken to the hospital. Basham's companion, also arrested, was shown a picture of Tollett, and he confirmed that the name "Basham" was an alias. Agents then positively identified Tollett, but it was not until the next day that Tollett regained consciousness and admitted his true identity. Tollett was moved from the hospital to Alcatraz Penitentiary on June 9 and died there on June 14.

No. 14
FREDERICK J. TENUTO

First Most Wanted Listing:
May 24, 1950
Process Dismissed:
March 9, 1964

Some of the criminals on the Most Wanted List are never captured—but that doesn't mean that they are still at large.

Frederick Tenuto is one such fugitive. The last of Tenuto's scrapes with the law resulted in a ten- to twenty-year sentence on a charge of second-degree murder. In 1940 Tenuto and a companion had an argument with Dominic DeCaro and his father, James. Tenuto then shot and killed James DeCaro and seriously wounded Dominic.

On February 10, 1947, Tenuto and four other prisoners staged what the FBI called a "spectacular" prison break from the Holmesburg Penitentiary in Pennsylvania. According to the FBI, the five men pried open their cell doors with a stolen chisel and overpowered the guards. Using a guard as a shield, they obtained ropes and ladders from the boiler room. They then escaped over a wall under gunfire.

Three of the prisoners were recaptured within twenty-four hours. Another, Willie Sutton—who later also made the Most Wanted List—was recaptured two years later in New York City. Tenuto, however, was not captured—effecting the first successful break from the maximum security prison in over fifty years.

It was not likely they would have held him long anyway. In 1942, while imprisoned on the murder charge, Tenuto staged an escape with another inmate by constructing a ladder from threaded sections of pipe that they then used to scale the prison wall. To keep the guards from becoming suspicious, Tenuto and his companion made dummies from old clothes stuffed with towels and other material, then left them facing the wall on the bunks in their cells. False heads were made with brown paper, soap, and "hair" cut from a brush.

Their makeshift ladder, however, broke during the escape, and Tenuto injured his foot after a thirty-foot drop. He was apprehended along with his companion the following day.

Tenuto escaped again in the spring of 1945, this time by digging a tunnel over a period of eleven months. The tunnel, equipped with electric lights, led to the surface outside the prison wall. This time Tenuto eluded authorities for nearly two months before being recaptured in New York City.

The FBI release on Tenuto said: "Although quiet in manner, he is reported to commit crimes on the spur of the moment and has been known to stage a holdup for the purpose of obtaining beer money. He reportedly has boasted he does not intend to be taken alive. He is believed to be armed and should be considered extremely dangerous."

In 1964 the FBI announced that after "a long and vigorous" investigation, no trace of Tenuto had been found. "Recurrent rumors, however, were heard from the underworld that Tenuto was dead and had been unceremoniously buried in an inaccessible grave," the FBI said. With this information, Tenuto was removed from the Most Wanted List after the federal process against him had been dismissed.

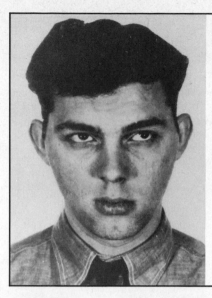

No. 18
JOSEPH F. BENT, JR.

First Most Wanted Listing:
January 9, 1951
Apprehended:
August 29, 1952

When a court ordered Joseph Bent, Jr., jailed for twenty-five years in 1949, it appeared that another veteran holdup man had been put away for good. But only months later, a court motion on Bent's earlier indictment led another judge to release him.

Did Bent get off scot-free? Still later, yet another federal court ruled that the original conviction should stand, and Bent was asked to return to the federal penitentiary at Leavenworth, Kansas. Bent, who was managing a fish market in Kansas City, Missouri, at the time, had other plans. He fled to California and vowed not to be taken alive.

It appeared he intended to keep his vow. On July 23, 1949, his face partly covered with adhesive tape, Bent entered a large grocery store in San Diego, California, and held up the cashiers, escaping with $2,150 in a getaway car driven by a companion.

The robbers were spotted by a motorcycle officer at a San Diego intersection. During a chase, both Bent and the officer fired upon each other, but the two robbers eluded police. The next day, Bent's companion was arrested, and an alert was put out for Bent.

In order to escape arrest at a bus station in Santa Barbara, Bent stole a car, but he wrecked it on the highway. Then, although he was slightly injured, he walked off the road into the sagebrush, leaving a bloody trail behind him. Even though the temperature was 105 degrees, authorities trailing Bent found only his discarded clothing.

The search for Bent continued, but it was his picture in the August 1952 issue of *Parade* magazine that brought a telephone call to the FBI in Alaska.

There, a citizen said that the photograph was that of a man who had previously resided in Monterey, Mexico. An inquiry in Monterey then led to Texas City, Texas, where Bent was located in an apartment.

Still unwilling to give himself up, Bent ran from the agents, and when, according to the FBI, he made a menacing motion and appeared to be drawing a gun, an agent stopped him with a shot in the thigh. Even then, Bent still offered fierce resistance to arrest, but he was finally captured and returned to Leavenworth.

No. 22
FREDERICK E. PETERS

First Most Wanted Listing:
July 2, 1951
Apprehended:
January 15, 1952

Many desperate fugitives pull out firearms when cornered. Others pull out lies and try to trick law enforcement agents. Frederick Peters ranks near the top of the list among the many liars the FBI has encountered.

Wanted for interstate transportation of stolen property, impersonation, and probation violation, Peters attracted the attention of two FBI agents in a Washington, D.C., hotel lobby on January 15, 1952, a little over six months after he had been placed on the Most Wanted List.

One of the agents noticed his strong resemblance to the man the List described as Peters. The other agent agreed with him. When approached, the man identified himself as Paul Carpenter and said that he was hurrying to an important appointment at the State Department to discuss the production of a music festival in Montevideo, Uruguay.

When "Carpenter" insisted on keeping his appointment, the agents accompanied him to the State Department. When they arrived there, he said that the appointment was actually at the Pan-American Union. Finally, he consented to be fingerprinted. He admitted his real name after he had been identified as Peters by the prints.

No. 23
ERNEST TAIT

First Most Wanted Listing:
July 11, 1951
Apprehended:
July 12, 1951

There is nothing quite as likely to cause indigestion as finding your Most Wanted photograph in a newspaper while you are eating. That's exactly what happened to Ernest Tait on the night of July 11, 1951. Sitting in a restaurant in Coral Gables, Florida, while dining on fried chicken, Tait saw a photograph of himself with a caption identifying him as a Most Wanted fugitive. He quickly folded up the newspaper and abandoned his dinner.

Only hours later, the restaurant manager opened another copy of the paper and recognized his former customer. The next day, the FBI received two phone calls, both from local merchants, who said that Tait—sought for unlawful flight to avoid prosecution for burglary—had visited their stores recently and used the name J. Marsh.

Following other leads, the FBI determined the fugitive was driving a 1951 Oldsmobile, but none of the area automobile dealers recognized Tait. Only twenty minutes after agents had left one Oldsmobile agency, a man driving a '51 Olds came in and asked for a grease job.

Service attendants recognized the man as Tait. While one hoisted the car onto the rack to make sure their customer could not escape, another called the FBI, and agents were promptly dispatched to the scene. Tait was arrested without incident, but it was determined that he had two .45 caliber pistols in his car—still sitting high over the garage floor.

No. 34
LEONARD JOSEPH ZALUTSKY

First Most Wanted Listing:
August 5, 1952
Apprehended:
September 8, 1952

Leonard Zalutsky was serving a life term in prison for the murder of a Miami police officer when he decided that he had had enough. Using flaming gasoline bombs, he escaped from the Florida State Prison on September 3, 1951. Less than a year later, he was added to the Most Wanted List.

Far away from his escape point, Zalutsky's photograph caught the attention of two residents of Beaver Falls, Pennsylvania, who were studying a wanted poster in the local post office.

They contacted the police and reported that the fugitive on the poster resembled a man living in the area who had been working under the name of Dominic Bulaski.

Police went to a local hospital where Bulaski had worked and were given his previous address. During their visit who should happen to arrive but Bulaski. After being identified by his fingerprints, Bulaski finally admitted that he was Zalutsky, saying that he had been living a very orderly life in Beaver Falls to avoid suspicion.

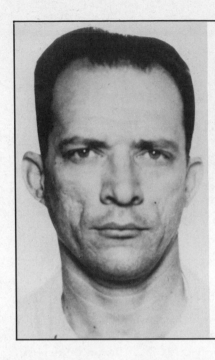

No. 37 and No. 94
NICK GEORGE MONTOS

First Most Wanted Listing:
September 8, 1952
Apprehended:
August 23, 1954

Second Most Wanted Listing:
March 2, 1956
Apprehended:
March 28, 1956

Montos became the first individual to make the FBI's Most Wanted List twice. His first entry came after the brutal robbery and beating of two elderly people in Georgia and the $150,000 robbery of a Wisconsin art dealer. Captured and sentenced to seven years in a Mississippi prison for a safe burglary, Montos made the List for the second time after escaping from prison—his fifth such escape. A few weeks after his second listing, he was arrested in a Memphis motel room loaded with weapons, including a submachine gun.

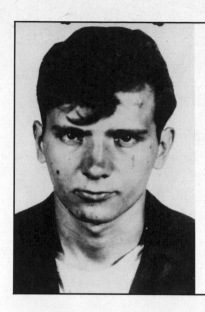

No. 43
JOSEPH JAMES BRLETIC

First Most Wanted Listing:
February 9, 1953
Apprehended:
February 10, 1953

In June 1948 Joseph Brletic was arrested in St. Louis, Missouri, after a crime spree that included six robberies in a matter of months in Pennsylvania and still another in Missouri.

No one could hold onto Brletic long. Three months later, the twenty-four-year-old criminal and a companion cut through a wall with a pair of stolen barber's shears and clawed their way out of the St. Louis County Jail. According to authorities, Brletic then headed west by hopping rides on freight trains.

The FBI's Most Wanted poster listed Brletic's physical characteristics and his past activities: "Investigation has shown that this criminal, posing under the alias of Frank Garfolo, worked as a pin boy at bowling alleys and as a gambling 'shill' at gambling places in Las Vegas."

It was the bowling reference on his poster that struck Brletic out. When his picture was published in the *Los Angeles Herald Express,* a citizen recognized him as "James Rizzo," who was working as a pinsetter at a bowling alley and had married a Lancaster, California, woman. Local authorities found and arrested Brletic without incident.

No. 49
JOSEPH LEVY

First Most Wanted Listing:
May 1, 1953
Apprehended:
April 30, 1953

Joseph Levy holds some sort of record for the shortest non-stay on the Most Wanted List.

The search for Levy began in March 1951; he was wanted on charges of interstate transportation of stolen property and probation violation. Plans were made to add Levy to the Most Wanted List on May 1, 1953, and photographs and descriptions of him were released to FBI agents in advance, in anticipation of the listing.

But before the List was released to the public, two agents who were seeking another fugitive spotted Levy at a fifty-dollar betting window at Churchill Downs Race Track in Louisville, Kentucky. Following Levy to a nearby paddock, they saw him give twenty dollars to a tipster. The agents then took Levy into custody without incident.

Levy denied his identity, claiming his name was Morris Goldsmith and displaying identification in that name. But the agents were not fooled, and Levy finally admitted his true identity, adding, "When you dance, you have to pay the piper, and this is the end of the road for me."

No. 62
THOMAS JACKSON MASSINGALE

First Most Wanted Listing:
November 18, 1953
Apprehended:
November 26, 1953

After a brutal escape from prison, Thomas Massingale began making a good living as a photograph salesman. Ironically, a photograph published in a magazine also brought an abrupt end to his new career.

Imprisoned at the Kansas State Industrial Reformatory in Hutchinson, Kansas, he and two companions assaulted two guards with a butcher knife and club and fled in a commandeered automobile, taking one of the guards as a hostage. Shortly afterward, Massingale's companions were captured, but he eluded authorities.

He was placed on the Most Wanted List on November 18, 1953, and a Wyoming resident recognized his picture in the *Saturday Evening Post* on November 24 and contacted the FBI. At the time of his arrest, Massingale said he was working as a photograph salesman, earning more than a hundred dollars per week. He claimed he was so successful that he was slated to become a manager within a short time. He also said, "It's been a good run," but complained to FBI agents about the "notoriety" given to him by the Most Wanted program.

No. 65
CHESTER LEE DAVENPORT

First Most Wanted Listing:
January 6, 1954
Apprehended:
January 7, 1954

Chester Davenport was proficient at two criminal activities—rustling and jail breaks, and for a while it looked as if no prison could hold him very long.

Davenport and his brother Norman first came to the attention of law enforcement authorities during the investigation of an extensive cattle theft ring in the Midwest. On February 13, 1951, an inquisitive state highway patrolman stopped two men in a cattle truck near Peggs, Oklahoma. The two men brandished guns and took a revolver and shotgun from the police car. They forced the trooper to accompany them but released him in the vicinity of Locust Grove. The Davenports were identified as the rustlers. A manhunt was launched, but a heavy snowstorm hampered the police.

Six days later, the Davenport brothers were captured by the highway patrol while driving in a car belonging to yet another hostage.

Jailed in Pryor, Oklahoma, the Davenports overpowered the Mayes County jailer, then robbed him of his pistol and automobile. They abandoned his car and, commandeering another, forced the owner to drive them to Texas. After a concerted effort by the FBI and local detectives, Chester Davenport was arrested that March in Wichita Falls, Kansas. Norman Davenport surrendered days later.

Chester Davenport was convicted of armed robbery, and on May 2, 1951, he began serving a twenty-five-year sentence. On July 4, 1953, he celebrated Independence Day by escaping from prison.

Davenport fled to California, where he found work as a laborer on a dairy farm. When he was added to the Most Wanted List on January 6, 1954, his picture was printed in a local newspaper. The photograph drew the attention of a doctor who frequently visited the farm where Davenport worked, and he told the police that the picture was of a man calling himself Floyd D. Tucker. FBI agents, accompanied by police and sheriff's deputies, then surrounded a barn on the farm and arrested Davenport without incident.

Davenport's employer, however, said that he would "take him back tomorrow if he was put on parole right now. If that man was given a break, I think he'd make something of himself." But Davenport was returned to an Oklahoma prison.

No. 71
BASIL KINGSLEY BECK

First Most Wanted Listing:
March 1, 1954
Apprehended:
March 3, 1954

The FBI wished Basil Beck "happy birthday" on March 1, 1954, by placing the just-turned twenty-one-year-old on the Most Wanted List. While some people might have thought the Bureau's gift poorly timed, Beck's life story shows that he received an appropriate birthday present.

A runaway at eleven, burglar at thirteen, escapee from state training school at fourteen, and convict at eighteen, Beck violated his parole by the time he was twenty. The FBI began taking an interest in Beck after he and three other inmates staged a jailbreak in Oswego, Kansas, on September 5, 1953, overpowering a jailer and deputy and taking their guns and an automobile.

Beck's long escape trail led through Missouri, Arkansas, Pennsylvania, New Jersey, Michigan, South Dakota, Wyoming, and California. In Joplin, Missouri, he and his companions stole another automobile, which was later found abandoned in Arkansas. There, Beck became separated from the other escapees, who subsequently engaged in a gun battle with police that ended with one fugitive dead and the others in custody.

Beck, meanwhile, was spotted in Philadelphia with an attorney. The man was found beaten to death afterward.

When Beck made the Most Wanted List, leads began pouring in, and the FBI traced him to San Pablo, California. He was arrested there on March 3, 1954, only two days after his birthday. Under questioning, Beck admitted to burglaries in Wisconsin, Kansas, Oklahoma, and California during the period of his freedom.

No. 76
JOHN ALFRED HOPKINS

First Most Wanted Listing:
May 18, 1954
Apprehended:
June 7, 1954

John Hopkins called the period after his escape from the Arizona State Penitentiary a "vacation." He didn't consult a travel guide to determine the best spots to visit—he checked the local post offices, and whenever he happened upon a picture of himself on a wanted poster, he would hightail out of town.

On November 30, 1953, the date of his jailbreak, Hopkins was serving a life sentence for the murder of a policeman who had surprised him during a burglary. After he escaped, Hopkins said, he spent most of his time near Watsonville, California. But after he was added to the Most Wanted List in May 1954, one of his daily checks at the post office confirmed his worst fears. He tore the Most Wanted poster from the wall and swiftly left town.

While he had wanted to head for Salt Lake City, Utah, he decided on Reno, Nevada, when he found out that the FBI maintained an office in Salt Lake City. In Reno, however, he again found his picture hanging on the post office wall. It was in Elko, Nevada, where there was no photograph in the post office, that Hopkins felt he had finally found his refuge.

But local citizens recognized Hopkins's photograph in a newspaper, and he was arrested in a mining area near Beowawe, Nevada. Upon his capture, he said that during his "vacation" he felt "condemned to capture." He also commented that he had frequently eaten thick steaks to "bolster his constitution" since he anticipated meager rations upon his return to prison.

No. 81
GEORGE LESTER BELEW

First Most Wanted Listing:
January 4, 1955
Apprehended:
January 24, 1955

If George Belew hadn't chosen to pass worthless checks for his living, he might have been able to write a travel guide to the United States. In fact, Belew—described as friendly and smooth in manner—once posed as a writer collecting material for a book.

According to the FBI, Belew began his career early; in July 1931, when he was only seventeen, he was sentenced to ten years for forgery at the Iowa State Reformatory at Anamosa.

Paroled in 1935, Belew led a rather nomadic life. In following years, he was jailed again in Iowa for forgery; in Canada for false pretenses with intent to defraud; in Georgia for interstate car theft and transporting counterfeit securities in interstate commerce; and in Washington as a conditional release violator.

Released from the federal penitentiary at McNeil Island in Washington on February 6, 1953, he was charged three weeks later with passing fraudulent checks in North Dakota.

Belew was arrested on July 30, 1954, in Hays, Kansas, but escaped four days later after assaulting a jailer. Belew and a companion blinded the guard with hot soapy water when he brought them their breakfast. Using an iron bar ripped from the cell bunk, Belew struck the man on the head, then stripped him of his wallet and keys before stealing a police car.

This was at least the third successful break from prison for Belew. He had once apparently plotted another escape: he ate soap to produce a fever and bit his tongue to show blood in an unsuccessful attempt to be admitted to the prison hospital, from which, presumably, he would have tried to free himself again.

Belew was finally apprehended on January 24, 1955, when he registered at a motel near Champaign, Illinois, under the name of Dr. Claude C. Hoyt. The proprietor, however, had recently received a Most Wanted poster with Belew's photograph and description, and he notified the authorities.

The FBI's description of Belew was extremely detailed, leaving little to the imagination: "According to acquaintances, this fugitive drinks alcoholic beverages and likes beer, preferably Budweiser, and smokes cigarettes, favoring Camels or king-size Embassy. He is fond of fried chicken drumsticks and thighs, drinks coffee without cream, has French toast as his choice breakfast, and enjoys banana cream pie as his favorite dessert. Fishing is his principal hobby, but he is also very interested in textile painting, poetry, and script writing."

FBI agents and local authorities confronted "Dr. Hoyt," who produced calling cards, as well as an application for an Illinois driver's license, all in that name. However, the suspect had tatoos identical to Belew's, including a faded scroll on his upper right arm, two roses, the inscription "Mother Rose of My" and a heart pierced with a dagger, and the words "Death Before Dishonor." After an interview Belew admitted who he really was.

In his possession at the time of his arrest, Belew had a small gray metal box containing rubber stamps, identification cards, blank check forms, and other essential tools of the fraudulent check trade.

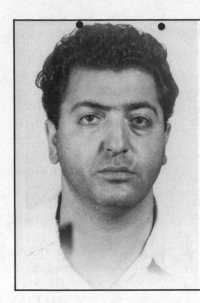

No. 98
CARMINE DIBIASE

First Most Wanted Listing:
May 28, 1956
Apprehended:
August 28, 1958

It was the Christmas season and Michael Erreciello had been the best man at Carmine DiBiase's wedding. But that didn't stop DiBiase on December 26, 1951, when he walked into a New York social club and pumped four bullets into Erreciello, who was sleeping in a chair.

Following the shooting, DiBiase was said to have turned to one of his two companions and ordered him to kill a second man with the victim. But the gun jammed and the man escaped.

DiBiase was added to the Most Wanted List on May 28, 1956. Over two years later, a well-dressed DiBiase surrendered to the FBI through an attorney.

"I feel a million times better," DiBiase said after his surrender. "I am getting older and accomplishing nothing having to stay away from my wife and children, mother and father. I am glad it is over. I had to come in."

No. 105 and No. 188
QUAY CLEON KILBURN

First Most Wanted Listing:
April 16, 1958
Apprehended:
June 2, 1958

Second Most Wanted Listing:
March 23, 1964
Apprehended:
June 25, 1964

The power of the press had already put plenty of Most Wanted fugitives behind bars, but Quay Kilburn let the media help him *escape* from jail, with no need for a ladder or a saw. Behind bars in Utah State Prison for violation of earlier parole conditions, he was also serving as the editor of the prison paper. Kilburn used his "press card" on the pretense of interviewing prisoners outside the prison walls. Once outside, he fled.

An alert citizen recognized a published photograph of Kilburn, and he was arrested without incident in Los Angeles on June 2, 1958.

Paroled in 1963, he was charged only months later with cashing a number of fraudulent checks in Salt Lake City. Kilburn was placed on the Most Wanted List again—the fourth fugitive to make the list twice. He was apprehended for the second time on June 25, 1964, in a parking lot. Although he was armed with a .32 caliber revolver, an agents' report said he was given no chance to resist.

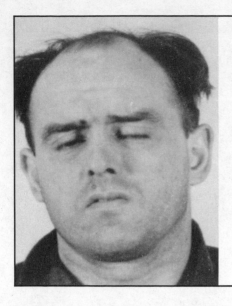

No. 109
FRANK LAWRENCE SPRENZ

First Most Wanted Listing:
September 10, 1958
Apprehended:
April 15, 1959

The FBI's apprehension report minced no words about Frank Sprenz, quoting Director J. Edgar Hoover as saying he was "as daring a desperado as ever appeared on the roster of the 'Top Ten' bad men."

Whereas most fugitives limited their escape vehicles to automobiles, Sprenz parlayed flying lessons and an ability to change his physical appearance into more than half a year of freedom.

During that time Sprenz hardly laid low. He chalked up nearly $26,000 from a spree of bank robberies and stole several airplanes and cars.

Twenty-nine at the time of his arrest, Sprenz had a long history of criminal involvement. The FBI put it this way: "Sprenz, as revealed by his past record, has been a menace most to life and property since he was a juvenile." His first arrest, for auto theft, was at the age of fifteen.

Sprenz first came to the attention of the FBI in 1947 when he admitted to having stolen a machine gun from an armed forces base at Aberdeen, Maryland, where he was assigned after enlisting five months before. He also admitted that he stole a .45 caliber pistol.

Sprenz finally graduated to the Most Wanted List on September 10, 1958, several months after a spectacular escape from the Summit County Jail in Akron, Ohio, where he had been imprisoned awaiting a trial on robbery charges. Two months after his arrest, Sprenz opened his cell-block door with a homemade key fashioned from the metal springs of his bunk. With four accomplices he surprised the inside guard and threw scalding-hot coffee in his face before the man could sound the alarm.

Continuing their rampage in the jail, the five men overpowered several deputy sheriffs, stole two revolvers and a riot gun, and fled to the nearby county garage, where they took possession of two cars. Unable to open the garage doors, they rammed the cars through them and drove off.

One car was located quickly. One escapee surrendered, while another was killed by police after holding a family at gunpoint. Within several weeks all the men were apprehended—except Sprenz, who was then added to the Most Wanted List.

On March 2, 1959, Sprenz was reported to have robbed a bank in Hamilton, Ohio. He fled in a car with stolen plates and drove to a nearby airport, where he stole a getaway plane. The FBI said that Sprenz "has had but basic flying instructions" but that the escape plane was the third airplane he had stolen.

Sprenz was finally located and arrested by the Mexican Federal Security Police and the Yucatán State Police on the island of Cozumel. The Mexican police said that when he was arrested, Sprenz was carrying a handbag loaded with $20,000 in cash. Officers found two loaded revolvers in the dirt-floored grass hut where, they said, Sprenz had been living since April 4, 1959.

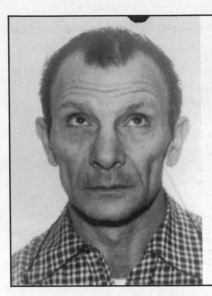

No. 121
FREDERICK ANTHONY SENO

First Most Wanted Listing:
September 24, 1959
Apprehended:
September 24, 1959

Most fugitives on the run from the FBI lurk in the shadows and fringes of society to remain anonymous, but Frederick Seno didn't try very hard.

Arrested for the robbery at gunpoint of a Chicago supermarket, he escaped from a Cook County, Illinois, courtroom shortly before his trial on December 11, 1958.

Seno was added to the FBI's Most Wanted List on September 24, 1959. On the same day agents tracked him to a rooming house in Miami, Florida, where he was living under the name of Victor Rose. "Don't shoot, don't shoot," Seno shouted at FBI agents who approached him.

What had Seno been doing for the nine months he was on the run? He claimed he had been working in Miami as a chef and a caterer and that he had catered parties for many prominent people in the area.

The 1950s
Rogues' Gallery

No. 29
SYDNEY GORDON MARTIN

First Most Wanted Listing:
January 7, 1952
Apprehended:
November 27, 1953

After asking a Massachusetts farmer for help with his stalled automobile, Martin turned on him with a gun and demanded money. When the farmer moved to get off his tractor, he was shot twice in the chest, then bashed on the head with a rock several times. The farmer survived, and Martin was indicted on charges of assault with intent to murder.

No. 30
GERHARD ARTHUR PUFF

First Most Wanted Listing:
January 28, 1952
Apprehended:
July 26, 1952

Wanted for the armed robbery of $62,000 from a Kansas bank in 1951.

No. 31
THOMAS EDWARD YOUNG

First Most Wanted Listing:
February 21, 1952
Apprehended:
September 23, 1952

Wanted on five separate charges including bank robbery, escape, and transportation of stolen vehicles.

No. 32
KENNETH LEE MAURER

First Most Wanted Listing:
February 27, 1952
Apprehended:
January 8, 1953

Wanted for the brutal murders of his eleven-year-old sister, whom he stabbed four times, and his mother, who suffered two skull fractures and thirty-six cuts and stab wounds.

No. 36
JAMES EDDIE DIGGS

First Most Wanted Listing:
August 27, 1952
Apprehended:
December 14, 1961

Wanted for the gunshot murders of Ruth Outlaw Diggs and her two sons, James Diggs, Junior, six, and Alfonso Diggs, four. Two shots were fired into the woman's body and three shots into the bodies of each of the children.

No. 38
THEODORE RICHARD BYRD, JR.

First Most Wanted Listing:
September 10, 1952
Apprehended:
August 21, 1954

Wanted for interstate transportation of stolen property after he obtained over $40,000 by cashing fraudulent checks in the Southwest and Midwest.

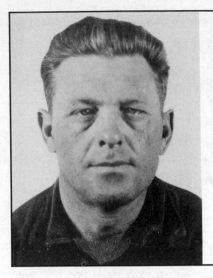

No. 50
ARNOLD HINSON

First Most Wanted Listing:
May 4, 1953
Apprehended:
November 7, 1953

Described by the FBI as a "nomadic car thief," Hinson was added to the FBI's Most Wanted List after the body of a Montana ranch hand, with four bullet holes in the head, was found in a field. The victim had last been seen with Hinson and his wife.

No. 51
GORDON LEE
COOPER

First Most Wanted Listing:
May 11, 1953
Apprehended:
June 11, 1953

Wanted on charges of unlawful flight to avoid prosecution for robbery. An escapee from a Missouri penitentiary, he and another jailmate accosted a guard, beat him with a homemade blackjack, and robbed him of money and personal belongings.

No. 52
FLEET ROBERT CURRENT

First Most Wanted Listing:
May 18, 1953
Apprehended:
July 12, 1953

Wanted after a bookkeeper of a San Francisco restaurant was robbed en route to the bank while carrying $1,495.07 in two canvas bags.

No. 53
DONALD CHARLES FITTERER

First Most Wanted Listing:
June 8, 1953
Apprehended:
June 21, 1953

Wanted for murder after the bullet-riddled body of a Midwest man was found in the underbrush near Denmark, Iowa. It was determined that Fitterer and a companion had met the man only hours earlier in a Gulf Port, Illinois, tavern.

No. 57
GEORGE WILLIAM KRENDICH

First Most Wanted Listing:
July 27, 1953
Apprehended:
October 11, 1953

Wanted for murder following the discovery of the partially decomposed, mutilated body of a pregnant woman, found partially submerged in a creek in Kentucky. Later that year, Krendich himself was found sitting behind the wheel of a jeep with the exhaust pipe extended through one of the vehicle's tightly fitted side curtains. His body was so badly decomposed that it was necessary for portions of the skin on the fingertips to be examined in the FBI laboratory before he could be identified.

No. 67
EVERETT LOWELL KRUEGER

First Most Wanted Listing:
January 25, 1954
Apprehended:
February 15, 1954

The FBI joined the search for Krueger, a prison escapee, after he used a stolen vehicle to cross state lines during his flight from the Teton County Jail in Jackson, Wyoming.

No. 69
NELSON ROBERT DUNCAN

First Most Wanted Listing:
February 8, 1954
Apprehended:
February 21, 1954

Wanted on the basis of three separate charges, including interstate transportation of an automobile, unlawful flight to avoid prosecution for robbery, and transporting a firearm with an obliterated serial number.

No. 70
CHARLES FALZONE

First Most Wanted Listing:
February 24, 1954
Apprehended:
August 17, 1955

Wanted after robbing a Tonawanda, New York, boat company payroll—more than $6,000—from two fellow employees in 1947.

No. 73
CLARENCE "JOCK" DYE

First Most Wanted Listing:
March 8, 1954
Apprehended:
August 3, 1955

Wanted after fleeing to avoid prosecution for two desperate holdups at gunpoint in Akron, Ohio, in 1946.

No. 75
RAYMOND LOUIS OWEN MENARD

First Most Wanted Listing:
May 3, 1954
Apprehended:
May 5, 1954

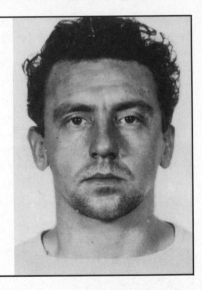

The FBI's detailed description of Menard helped in apprehending this alley gang member who had taken part in numerous robberies and burglaries. Information released on Menard described his habit of wearing sports clothes, and his wife's former occupation as a nightclub entertainer and dancer. When a New Orleans newspaper reader recognized his description, Menard, wearing flashy sports clothes, and his wife, who was employed at the time as a nightclub dancer, were arrested at their New Orleans apartment only days after making the Most Wanted List.

No. 77
OTTO AUSTIN LOEL

First Most Wanted Listing:
May 21, 1954
Apprehended:
January 17, 1955

An alert was put out to locals of the International Molders and Foundry Workers of North America when Loel fled following the brutal stabbing murder of a woman in an Oklahoma City motel. The FBI theorized that Loel, a skilled foundry worker, might try to rejoin the union under his own name or an alias.

No. 78
DAVID DANIEL KEEGAN

First Most Wanted Listing:
June 21, 1954
Apprehended:
December 13, 1963

Wanted for his part in the murder of a fifty-one-year-old farmer near Mondamin, Iowa. Wearing masks, Keegan and two other men broke into the farmhouse and ordered the farmer to open a safe. When the victim scuffled with the ringleader of the trio, he was felled by two of three bullets fired from the leader's gun, then left to die on the floor.

No. 80
JOHN HARRY ALLEN

First Most Wanted Listing:
September 7, 1954
Apprehended:
December 21, 1954

An "escape artist" according to the FBI, Allen escaped from penitentiaries in Tennessee, Alabama, North Dakota, and Kansas. He was wanted for unlawful flight to avoid prosecution for the crime of armed robbery.

No. 86
GARLAND WILLIAMS DANIELS

First Most Wanted Listing:
February 18, 1955
Apprehended:
March 29, 1955

Wanted by the FBI after passing bad checks and escaping from federal prison.

No. 87
DANIEL WILLIAM O'CONNOR

First Most Wanted Listing:
April 11, 1955
Apprehended:
December 26, 1955

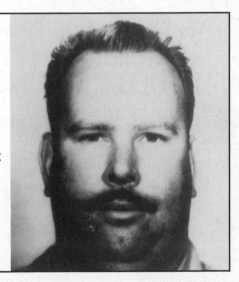

Wanted for desertion from the military and passing bad checks, O'Connor was also sought by the Canadian authorities on a charge of attempted murder in connection with an assault upon a Royal Canadian Mounted Police officer.

No. 97
EUGENE FRANCIS NEWMAN

First Most Wanted Listing:
May 28, 1956
Apprehended:
June 11, 1965

Newman allegedly fired a machine gun and wounded a guard during a botched attempt to rob an armored truck of racetrack revenues totaling $498,500.

No. 99
BEN GOLDEN MCCOLLUM

First Most Wanted Listing:
January 4, 1957
Apprehended:
March 7, 1958

While serving a prison sentence for robbery, McCollum became involved in a fight with two inmates. The FBI report said, "This terrible fight was observed by an eye witness. McCollum's assault upon the two fellow inmates was so fierce and ruthless that it was almost impossible to describe. Using an ugly, long-bladed knife, this killer cut the two inmates into ribbons

—both received gaping knife wounds in the stomach." He later escaped after being given permission to enter the prison hospital. The FBI then joined the search.

No. 100
ALFRED JAMES WHITE

First Most Wanted Listing:
January 14, 1957
Apprehended:
January 24, 1957

Surprised by a member of the West Virginia State Police while burglarizing a lumberyard in West Hamlin, West Virginia, White sprang from a darkened building and began firing at the officer. He then jumped into a nearby river and escaped.

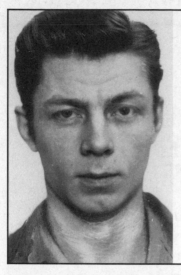

No. 101
ROBERT L. GREEN

First Most Wanted Listing:
February 11, 1957
Apprehended:
February 13, 1957

Imprisoned after being convicted of burglary, Green and a fellow inmate escaped from the Utah State Prison. Scaling a guard fence and diving into an irrigation ditch, they fled amid a hail of gunfire.

No. 102
GEORGE EDWARD COLE

First Most Wanted Listing:
February 25, 1957
Apprehended:
July 6, 1959

Wanted for the murder of a San Francisco police officer, Cole was arrested when a druggist in Des Moines, Iowa, recognized his female companion.

No. 104
FRANK AUBREY LEFTWICH

First Most Wanted Listing:
April 4, 1958
Apprehended:
April 18, 1958

Wanted for unlawful flight to avoid confinement, Leftwich opened fire on two police officers who had arrested him for drunk driving on May 21, 1950, in Lumberton, North Carolina. After he was found guilty of assault with intent to kill, Leftwich escaped from a North Carolina prison camp while serving a six- to ten-year sentence.

No. 106
DOMINICK SCIALO

First Most Wanted Listing:
May 9, 1958
Apprehended:
July 27, 1959

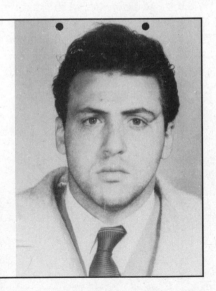

Scialo was wanted for unlawful flight to avoid prosecution for murder. The FBI said that Scialo fancied himself a "ladies' man" and that he was a good dancer who liked to patronize dance halls. It also said he "reportedly must refrain from drinking heavily and eating spicy foods due to injury of his liver caused by gunshot."

No. 107
ANGELO LUIGI PERO

First Most Wanted Listing:
June 16, 1958
Apprehended:
December 2, 1960

Wanted for the brutal murder of an aspiring seventeen-year-old boxer. A passerby found the victim crying for help in a Brooklyn gutter. Seeing the victim had been shot in the chest, the passerby went to call an ambulance in a nearby candy store. While in the store, he heard three loud reports. When he returned, a witness said that a car had drawn up beside the victim and someone had leaned out and fired three shots into the helpless body. The young man died a few days later.

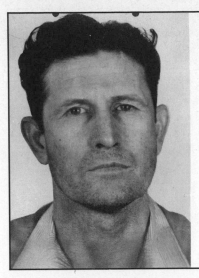

No. 111
JOHN THOMAS FREEMAN

First Most Wanted Listing:
February 17, 1959
Apprehended:
February 18, 1959

Wanted for a series of robberies and interstate transportation of a stolen vehicle. Freeman's alleged companion in crime was later found in a wooded area in Florida. He had been strangled, his throat had been cut from ear to ear, and he had been shot once through the head. In addition, medical examination showed that his entire midsection had been crushed.

No. 113
EMMETT BERNARD KERVAN

First Most Wanted Listing:
March 29, 1959
Apprehended:
May 13, 1959

Wanted for a 1959 robbery in which $29,445 was taken from a Connecticut bank, Kervan was arrested wearing his pajamas in a garage apartment in El Paso, Texas.

No. 114
RICHARD ALLAN HUNT

First Most Wanted Listing:
May 27, 1959
Apprehended:
June 2, 1959

With a list of charges pending against him, Hunt kidnaped one police officer and shot and critically wounded another.

No. 117
JAMES FRANCIS JENKINS

First Most Wanted Listing:
July 21, 1959
Apprehended:
August 12, 1959

Imprisoned in Philadelphia after robbing a bank of $17,730, Jenkins and two cellmates wormed their way through a narrow ceiling opening that they had dug with a smuggled screwdriver over thirteen days, and made good their escape.

The 1960s

Introduction

The 1960s saw the Most Wanted List at its most active—with 181 fugitives added during the decade. This era also signaled some of the List's most dramatic changes.

In 1968 the first "special addition" was named to the List: James Earl Ray, a small-time convict and prison escapee who was wanted in connection with the assassination of civil rights leader Rev. Dr. Martin Luther King, Jr.

The first woman to be named to the Most Wanted List was a product of the 1960s. Partners Ruth Eisemann-Schier and Gary Krist took part in one of the most spectacular kidnapings of all time, for which both were named to the List. Eisemann-Schier became number 293, and Krist number 292.

The Bureau had said years earlier that the closest a woman had come previously was Ruth Rose, a nineteen-year-old companion of Bobby Wilcoxson, entry number 167. Wilcoxson and his partner, Albert Nussbaum, number 168, were bank robbers extraordinaire. Despite not being named to the List, Rose was arrested on bank robbery charges.

Shortly after Eisemann-Schier had made the List, another woman was named Most Wanted. In fact, five out of the next twenty-three additions were women. One reason was the rise of radicalism connected to the national protests against the Vietnam War.

The Most Wanted List at the end of 1960s hinted at what the Most Wanted List of the 1970s would look like. On April 15, 1969, Cameron Bishop was named as number 300 on the Most Wanted List; he was sought in connection with the dynamiting of transmission towers supplying power to defense plants in Colorado.

No. 127
JOSEPH CORBETT, JR.

First Most Wanted Listing:
March 30, 1960
Apprehended:
October 29, 1960

There was no hint on the nearly five-page release that Joseph Corbett, Jr., was added to the FBI's Ten Most Wanted List for anything more than his escape from a California prison in 1955. While the FBI may not have put it in print, the media reported a sensational story: Joseph Corbett, Jr., was being sought in connection with the disappearance of millionaire Adolph Coors III.

Coors, board chairman of the Coors brewery in Golden, Colorado, became the object of an intensive search on February 9, 1960, when his station wagon was found abandoned with its motor running on a small rural bridge near his sprawling home in the Rocky Mountain foothills.

Bloodstains were found on the seat of the car and the bridge railing, and a pair of plastic-rimmed eyeglasses identified as Coors's were found in the shallow water of Turkey Creek, near the bridge.

Local authorities did not hesitate to say they felt that Coors had been kidnaped, and an intensive search of the surrounding area was launched, with 100 officers and volunteers participating.

The FBI was called immediately and joined in on the search for the forty-four-year-old father of four children. But no sign of Coors was found, and the day after the search began, the local sheriff said, "I'm still of the opinion he was taken out of the area yesterday, before he was even reported missing."

Wednesday's mail confirmed the fears of police and family. In it was a note demanding $500,000 in ransom. Mrs. Coors was to respond when the money was gathered by placing an ad in a local newspaper to advertise a tractor for sale.

While the family followed the kidnapers' instructions, no more contact was made, and law enforcement authorities were left to work with the clues they had discovered on the day of the crime. Follow-up investigations also uncovered what would prove to be another important clue: several local individuals reported seeing suspicious automobiles during the weeks preceding the crime near the spot where Coors was abducted.

The first hint the public had that the case might be near to being broken was the announcement on March 30, 1960, that thirty-one-year-old Joseph Corbett, Jr., a fugitive murderer living in nearby Denver, was being added to the Most Wanted List.

While the FBI refused to link Corbett's addition to the List directly with the Coors kidnaping, newspapers headlines read:

FBI Seeking Ex-Convict
Coors Case Suspect

Months later, authorities released more details about the case, but still refused to connect Corbett directly with the crime. They did, however, have these three things to say about Corbett: First, a man living under the name of Walter Osborne but identified later as Joseph Corbett disappeared from his Denver apartment less than twenty-four hours after Coors dropped from sight. Second, a week after Corbett's disappearance, a car identified as Corbett's was found blazing and abandoned in an Atlantic City, New Jersey, dump. Third, a foreman at Coors's home told police he had seen a yellow car that resembled Corbett's near the spot where Coors's car was found.

The FBI release on Corbett painted a picture of a man whom the agency called one of "considerable mystery." It went on to say he had been found guilty of second-degree murder of an air force sergeant who was killed by two gunshots to the head. Sentenced to a term of five years to life in 1951, Corbett broke out of the California Institution for Men at Chino in 1955. The FBI followed his trail to Glendale, California, and then to Denver, where he worked at a paint company.

The release went on to say that Corbett's associates had described him as "a normally calm, aloof individual who is capable of unusual mental development, but who becomes erratic when drinking. Prison psychiatrists have classified him as having a superior general intelligence but possibly having fantasies of omnipotence." The release also said that the fugitive had an interest in camping and firearms and had reportedly spent much of his time in Colorado's mountain areas engaging in target practice and the exploration of abandoned mines.

While family members remained optimistic that Coors would turn up, their hopes were finally dashed in September when clothing and human bones were found by a hiker on a remote mountain path twenty miles south of the Coors ranch. The clothes were identified by Coors's wife as those worn by her husband the day he was abducted. She also identified an initialed pocket knife found at the sight.

Details released shortly afterward revealed that the millionaire had been shot twice in the back and his body thrown on a mountain trash dump. At the same time, while not saying Corbett was a suspect, the FBI did disclose that he had boasted to his associates that he was planning a "big job"—one that would secure for him between a half- and one million dollars.

Nine months after the crime, Corbett was traced to a hotel room in Vancouver, Canada. Learning Corbett was expecting a delivery of a typewriter, FBI agents and local police knocked on the door and said they were deliverymen. As Corbett opened the door, he was met by drawn guns and gave up without a struggle.

Corbett maintained he was innocent but was found guilty of the murder and sentenced to life imprisonment in Colorado. In 1979, after nearly nineteen years in prison, Corbett was released. But he lasted only one day— jumping parole in California. He eventually turned himself in and, after spending another year in prison, was released to a halfway house in 1980, for a return to society in three to four months.

No. 154
RICHARD LAURENCE MARQUETTE

First Most Wanted Listing:
June 29, 1961
Apprehended:
June 30, 1961

One of the grisliest murders the city of Portland, Oregon, ever knew became the object of intense media coverage in the northwest United States.

In the small community of Santa Maria, California, a leaflet distributed by the FBI brought down the object of the manhunt. A Santa Maria construction firm employee saw the photo and recognized a recent part-time addition to the work force; the man turned out to be Richard Marquette, a "special addition" to the Most Wanted List who was wanted for the murder of a twenty-three-year-old housewife.

The victim had met Marquette in a Portland bar and gone to his home on the evening of June 4, 1961. She was reported missing by her husband, but it was four days later that parts of a female body were found in various spots around southeast Portland. Days later, fingerprints confirmed the body was that of the victim.

An investigation of the victim's movements the night of her death pointed to Marquette, and a search of his vacant home turned up more body parts in his refrigerator.

Marquette was later to tell FBI agents that he attempted to escape prosecution by fleeing first to Mexico, then hitchhiking back to California after his money ran out. One individual who picked Marquette up told him of some work available in his construction company, and the fugitive followed up by working for a time.

When one of the thousands of brochures the FBI had distributed nationwide on Marquette drew interest in the construction company, the FBI was notified and agents spread through the community. The FBI release on the apprehension said, "The intensive manhunt for Marquette was climaxed in a salvage store in Santa Maria where the desperate fugitive, who had grown a mustache to alter his appearance, had been working on a part-time basis."

Upon his capture, Marquette said, "I knew the FBI would get me sooner or later."

After his return to Portland, he led authorities to the remainder of the victim's body.

No. 158
JOHN GIBSON DILLON

First Most Wanted Listing:
September 1, 1961
Apprehended:
March 2, 1964

John Dillon's criminal career began at sixteen and included a series of offenses—it ended at the bottom of a fifteen-foot well on a remote farm near Chelsea, Oklahoma.

It was there that Dillon was found in 1964, years after being added to the FBI's List for failing to appear for sentencing after a conviction as the leader of a dope-peddling ring. Dillon, who was better known as Matt, faced a possible federal term of 190 years on eleven narcotics violations. His fourteen codefendants received total sentences of 246 years in prison.

According to the FBI, Dillon's brushes with the law began in 1931 and included convictions for auto theft, grand larceny, transporting a stolen automobile interstate, burglary, interstate transportation of fraudulent traveler's checks, and violation of federal narcotics laws. He had also attempted to run down an Oregon deputy sheriff with his automobile in 1955 while being questioned.

In 1964 an anonymous tip led authorities to a remote farm near Chelsea, Oklahoma. There, a badly decomposed body was found in a water-filled well. Wired to the feet and body were 200 pieces of well-drilling equipment. Identification of the body was established through comparison of dental charts. Authorities said that Dillon's body had been in the well over a year.

No. 162
FRANCIS LAVERNE BRANNAN

First Most Wanted Listing:
December 27, 1961
Apprehended:
January 17, 1962

"Come and get me, I'm tired of running," said the telephone caller to FBI agents in Miami. With those words, Francis Brannan, wanted for the murder of the seventy-two-year-old widow of a Presbyterian minister, surrendered.

Brannan, a thirty-six-year-old drifter with a long history of involvement with police, had been staying with a sister and brother-in-law in Rushville, Illinois. He became a suspect when it was learned he had left his sister's home two days before the body of the victim was discovered.

Missing also was the victim's car, which was found five days later in Springfield, Illinois. Few details of the murder were released, but police did say that the victim's body was found sprawling at the top of the basement stairway in her home. She had been shot twice with a shotgun, once in the left arm and once in the back. Police theorized that robbery had been the motive.

Brannan broke into tears upon hearing his sentence: from sixty-six to eighty-six years in the state penitentiary for the murder.

No. 167
BOBBY RANDELL WILCOXSON

First Most Wanted Listing:
February 23, 1962
Apprehended:
November 10, 1962

No. 168
ALBERT FREDERICK NUSSBAUM

First Most Wanted Listing:
April 2, 1962
Apprehended:
November 4, 1962

The partnership began with a friendship in the Chillicothe Reformatory in Ohio. It ended as one of the most famous tales since the FBI's Gangster Era.

Bobby Wilcoxson and Albert Nussbaum first became acquainted while serving time in the Ohio prison. Wilcoxson had an eighteen-month sentence for interstate transportation of a stolen car; Nussbaum was serving five years for the possession and transporting of a Thompson machine gun.

Shortly after both men were released from prison, their friendship turned into a working partnership that included legitimate businesses as well as a score of big-dollar bank robberies along the East Coast. Almost brilliant in their planning, at one time the pair set off a series of bombs in Washington, D.C., to test a theory that a diversion such as a bomb blast could be the perfect cover for a successful bank robbery. The blasts, in 1961, gripped the nation's capital and led to what was called the "mad bomber" scare.

Nussbaum was considered the brains of the operation. Besides planning the robberies, he set up two businesses, including a gun-collecting operation under an alias. At one point his "collection" grew to include two Lahti antitank rifles with ammunition, submachine guns, automatic pistols, hand grenades, and bulletproof vests.

Wilcoxson was the "brawn" of the operation. It was Wilcoxson who volunteered to kill a guard at the Lafayette National Bank in Brooklyn, New York, during a job they were planning. The pair had cased the bank in advance, and during apparently innocent conversations each had had with the guard, they asked him what he would do if the bank was robbed. The guard said he just might decide to shoot it out with any robbers.

On December 15, 1961, the two men and an accomplice entered the bank. Wilcoxson walked up to the guard and pumped machine-gun bullets into him, killing him. A customer, however, alerted police, and an officer soon appeared with his gun drawn. With a heavy glass door between them, he and Wilcoxson exchanged fire. But the officer's revolver was no match for the door and Wilcoxson's higher-powered machine gun. Hit by a bullet, he was thrown backward and put out of action. Later, it was discovered the bullet was stopped by the officer's badge. The job netted the trio a total of $32,763, of which the third member of the gang received less than $500.

The FBI, however, began closing in, and when the third member of the gang was arrested, he told the identities of the other two. When agents made an appointment to visit Nussbaum in January 1962, he fled. On February 23, 1962, Wilcoxson and Nussbaum were added to the FBI's Most Wanted List. The Bureau's bulletin called Nussbaum "a highly intelligent, heavily-armed, alleged bank robber." Wilcoxson was described as a "heavily-armed, trigger-happy and extremely dangerous alleged bank robber."

Under the strain of their fugitive status, the pair began quarreling, their jobs became less fruitful, and they finally broke up after a bank robbery in Pittsburgh that netted them $28,901.

Nussbaum headed to Mexico, then telephoned his wife and asked her to meet him in New York City. There, agents spotted Nussbaum, and in the high-speed chase that followed, over thirty law enforcement vehicles sped after him. He eventually pulled into a parking lot and dropped to the floor of the car, thinking authorities would miss him. He looked up, and found himself staring into the barrel of a shotgun. Nussbaum gave up peacefully, despite the fact that he was carrying two live hand grenades and a .22 caliber rifle with a silencer.

Wilcoxson was tracked to Baltimore, where he and his wife were living as "father" and "daughter." Agents located their home and, posing as friendly neighbors concerned about a flat tire, were able to take Wilcoxson without violence.

Wilcoxson was given a life sentence, Nussbaum forty years.

No. 185
SAMMIE CARL AMMONS

First Most Wanted Listing:
February 10, 1964
Apprehended:
May 15, 1964

After his arrest Sammie Ammons told police that his babysitter's two-year-old and four-year-old children died of natural causes and he had merely helped dispose of their bodies. But evidence pointed to strangulation as the cause of death for the two children, whose bodies were found September 2, 1963, in an abandoned septic tank near Crossville, Tennessee.

Five months later, Ammons was added to the Most Wanted List, charged with unlawful flight from Tennessee to avoid prosecution for forgery. But local authorities said they were seeking Ammons and the babysitter for the murder of the two children.

Ammons was reportedly traveling with his wife, their six children, and the babysitter. He and his wife were said to have used many aliases as they traveled through different states, writing and passing bad checks and victimizing small businesses and taverns.

Ammons, whom the FBI said frequented roller-skating rinks and had been a "ladies' man," had allegedly impersonated law enforcement officers on several occasions and had been known to wear a special officer's badge and carry a .38 caliber nickel-plated automatic pistol in a hip holster.

Ammons was captured by police after a high-speed chase in Alabama. After the arrest the mother of the two children said that the children died one by one when Ammons told her they would be taken away if she called a doctor to treat them.

No. 189
JOSEPH FRANCIS BRYAN, JR.

First Most Wanted Listing:
April 14, 1964
Apprehended:
April 28, 1964

When the FBI arrested Joseph Bryan, Jr., they were too late to help two victims of kidnaping and murder, but they may have saved the life of an eight-year-old Tennessee youth.

Bryan was arrested in a shopping mall on the outskirts of New Orleans. In the stolen car he was driving, an eight-year-old boy who had been reported missing a week earlier from his home in Humboldt, Tennessee, was found alive. The boy had been missing since he left his brother at a snack bar to go home for a baseball. His bicycle was found near the house.

The FBI's Most Wanted flyer on Bryan said that he "reportedly enjoys seeing small boys tied up and screaming" and described him as a "dangerous former mental patient . . . sought for the kidnap slaying of a ten-year-old Mt. Pleasant, South Carolina, boy who disappeared on February 27, 1964. The body of the young boy was discovered March 31, 1964, in a marshy wooded area near Hallandale, Fla."

In fact, the FBI warned authorities that Bryan, who had served sentences for burglary and auto theft, had twice escaped confinement, and had attempted suicide, was an avid gambler who frequented racetracks. FBI agents spotted Bryan driving a car stolen from a Kentucky racetrack.

Bryan struggled with agents who approached him, but was pinned to the pavement and arrested. Beside the young boy, a loaded .22 revolver was found in the car. After an emotional reunion with his parents, the young kidnaping victim seemed more upset over being kissed in public than with his ordeal.

Authorities retraced Bryan's route after his arrest and found the body of a missing seven-year-old Florida boy in a state palmetto grove.

No. 201 RAYMOND LAWRENCE WYNGAARD

First Most Wanted Listing:
October 5, 1964
Apprehended:
November 28, 1964

One of the last places authorities might have thought to look for fugitive Raymond Wyngaard was in a schoolroom. But that's where the escapee spent a good deal of his time while fleeing the law.

Wyngaard, who was fleeing prosecution on a Detroit armed robbery charge, was originally arrested in Los Angeles by the FBI on June 27, 1964. Wyngaard was returned to Detroit, and while being taken to a courtroom for arraignment, he and an accomplice escaped. They allegedly went on a three-day crime spree in the Detroit area, robbing a gun shop and supermarket, shooting a Detroit police officer, robbing ten occupants of an office building and assaulting one of the victims, and stealing three cars and abducting two motorists.

Wyngaard's accomplice was arrested near Dearborn, Michigan, on July 27. But Wyngaard, a Wisconsin native, returned to his home state and enrolled in a vocational school in Madison.

But when the FBI published Wyngaard's photograph on Most Wanted posters, he attempted to flee the area. FBI agents arrested him at gunpoint as he was leaving a taxi. Later, the taxi driver was said to have helped the agents with the arrest.

After his capture, Wyngaard said, "I've lived in Madison since August. I went to the vocational school until they started broadcasting my description and put out the posters, and I sorta ducked out of sight." School authorities said that Wyngaard had used the name Fred Rogers. He had enrolled in a welding course and also taken a short course for holiday sales clerks.

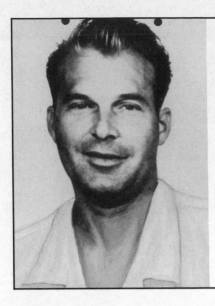

No. 203
JOHN WILLIAM CLOUSER

First Most Wanted Listing:
January 7, 1965
Process Dismissed:
August 1, 1972

The last thing most fugitives from the FBI want to do is keep in touch with the Bureau. John Clouser, however, was not the typical Most Wanted fugitive. He wrote the Bureau often and taunted them to "catch me if you can."

Clouser's FBI bulletin described him as "an armed and extremely dangerous escapee from a Florida mental hospital, who has vowed not to be taken alive. . . . Clouser, who reportedly termed himself the 'Florida Fox,' is currently charged with transporting a stolen motor vehicle between Georgia and Alabama, following his escape on April 2, 1964."

The Bureau said that Clouser and three other inmates fled from the mental ward of the Florida State Hospital in Chattahoochee. They then allegedly crossed the nearby state line into Georgia and, armed with a knife, accosted two hospital employees. The escapees reportedly forced their way into the car of one of the employees and forced the two to accompany them to the Columbus, Georgia, area. The hostages were robbed but released unharmed. The three inmates who accompanied Clouser were later apprehended, but he remained free for nine years.

A former police officer, Clouser resigned from the force in a Florida community in 1961 after being questioned about suspected participation in criminal offenses. Only a month after his resignation, he was arrested by the same department he had resigned from, and was charged with participation in the robbery, kidnaping, and beating of two Orlando, Florida, theater managers.

He was convicted and sentenced to thirty years in the Florida State Penitentiary, but he appealed the conviction and, because of a legal technicality, was released from prison and granted a new trial. He failed to show up for a court appearance and was later suspected of committing two burglaries and two armed robberies in which he brutally beat two of his victims.

Clouser was arrested in Knoxville, Tennessee, on September 29, 1963, and returned to Orlando, but he was adjudged legally insane and committed to the Florida State Hospital, from which he escaped. Years later, local police said Clouser had bragged to the deputy transporting him to the hospital about how he was able to convince the psychiatrists he was insane. "He was able to fool them," said a police official.

The police official said Clouser boasted of his cleverness in notes to the FBI, challenging the Bureau to catch him if it could. "I've heard he writes and tells them he was in such and such a place and they missed him there and maybe could get him the next place," the policeman said.

"Dear Mr. Hoover," one note from Clouser read, "Roses are red, violets are blue, your men aren't smart enough to catch me, so nuts to you."

The FBI's bulletin in circulation at the time of Clouser's placement on their Most Wanted List said he had been married three times, liked constant female companionship, and considered himself a "ladies' man." The Bureau said that acquaintances accused Clouser of being a braggart, a mama's boy, and a sadist who liked to start fights when drinking and would not hesitate to beat a victim to death. He reportedly liked to play poker, eat steaks, watch football and baseball games, and drink beer or bourbon whiskey.

The Bureau's description said that Clouser, though a blond, would often dye his hair black and wear a beard, wig, and mustache. They said he was known as a wearer of considerable jewelry and reportedly often had a brown wooden "tiki" doll on a chain around his neck.

The search for Clouser crossed the country, with the FBI in 1967 alerting fans who were to attend the Green Bay Packers game against the Los Angeles Rams in Milwaukee, Wisconsin, to keep their eyes open for the "avid professional football fan," who, the Bureau said, could possibly be in town to watch the game.

Despite numerous "sightings" in Milwaukee and elsewhere around the country, the Bureau did not catch Clouser and dropped him from the list when the federal process against him was dismissed in 1972.

Clouser, however, gave himself up two years later, negotiating through an attorney and surrendering to police on the front steps of the Florida Department of Criminal Law Enforcement Building in Tallahassee. He said at the time that he was "tired of running." He served only seven months of a five-year sentence for conspiracy in a robbery and was released on July 1, 1975. On that day his second wife divorced him, and a book was released about his life on the run.

No. 204
WALTER LEE PARMAN

First Most Wanted Listing:
January 15, 1965
Apprehended:
January 31, 1965

Walter Parman had two distinctly different experiences as a fugitive. The first lasted only a matter of weeks; the second lasted twelve years.

Parman was added to the Most Wanted List a few days after being named a suspect in the brutal strangulation murder of a thirty-two-year-old Washington, D.C., secretary, whose nude body was found in an alley in the nation's capital on January 9, 1965.

Parman later said that he had been dancing and drinking with the woman, then strangled her when she ridiculed him after he made advances to her in his apartment. Her body, which bore numerous bite marks, was identified through fingerprints.

Parman, who had previously been arrested for crimes in California, Texas, Colorado, Kansas, and the District of Columbia, was traced by the FBI to Los Angeles, where he was arrested. In his possession was a .25 caliber pistol together with a bank robbery "demand note."

Parman was sentenced to life in prison, but in 1972 he escaped from a guard while being escorted to an alleged speaking engagement at a Washington, D.C., university. Officials speculated that his getaway scheme involved a forged letter that appeared to extend him an invitation to speak.

In 1984, Parman was arrested again. At the time of his capture, he was employed as a manager for a high-tech company in San Francisco and described as "just your average employee."

A newspaper story written upon his arrest reported: " 'These last twelve years of my life were the happiest I ever had—until this,' said Walter Lee

Parman, as he sat Wednesday, surrounded by the mesh and metal of jail, looking like an old gray fox weary of the chase."

As the shipping and receiving manager of the computer disk drive manufacturer, Parman was in charge of testing incoming electrical and mechanical components. His salary was $50,000 at the time. He had been married in 1979 to a registered nurse he met at a neighborhood party.

He said he had checked the obituary pages of a newspaper for the year 1939, selected the name Mike Noble, then obtained a birth certificate, with which he applied for a driver's license and Social Security number. Authorities did not say how they traced him, but a fellow employee said, "Evidently someone spotted him at a seminar he'd attended on behalf of the company."

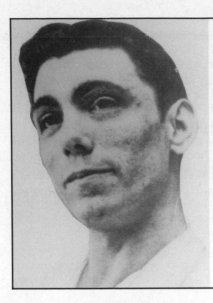

No. 211
LESLIE DOUGLAS ASHLEY

First Most Wanted Listing:
April 6, 1965
Apprehended:
April 23, 1965

Leslie Ashley, an escapee from a mental hospital who was once within hours of execution, would occasionally dress up as a woman. But when he was finally arrested, Ashley was playing the role of Bobo the Clown in a carnival.

Ashley had originally been arrested and tried after the brutal murder of a Houston real estate man. The victim had been shot six times with a .22 caliber revolver, and his body had then been dragged from his office, feet first, placed in a car, driven to a field, doused with gasoline, and ignited with a match. The body was so badly burned that the victim could only be identified through fingerprints.

Ashley, who had worked as a female impersonator in nightclubs that catered to homosexuals, was arrested in New York, where authorities found him dressed as a woman. He was prosecuted in Houston and found guilty. Sentenced to death in the electric chair, Ashley had his conviction reversed on an appeal. He was then declared insane—although sane at the time of the murder—and committed to a mental institution until he was sane enough to go on trial again.

He escaped from the maximum security ward of the Texas State Mental Hospital in San Antonio on October 6, 1964. His escape resulted in a hospital scandal in which several employees were fired.

After Ashley was named to the Most Wanted List, the FBI's release included a list of his nicknames: Douglas Ashley, Cookie Cordell, Edward Elizondo, Rose Goldberg, Ted Kipperman, C. D. LaMonte, Charles Scott, and Reneé.

Ashley hired on as Bobo the Clown for a carnival in Atlanta and spent three days working in clown makeup, sitting on a platform above a tank. Carnival patrons paid for the privilege of trying to knock him into four feet of water.

He was discovered by a fellow carnival worker, who happened to notice a wanted poster in Ashley's suitcase. That poster showed Ashley with a brunette wig on. "When I saw that wanted poster, we all dumbed up," said the worker. "Man, we acted like we don't know nothing. He had told us he was from Texas. And he acted a little bit like a mental patient. Funny, kind of."

He ended up contacting the FBI, which arrested Ashley. At the time of his arrest, he was wearing a white shirt and dark pants. Even Ashley's mother admitted she was "glad" her son had been captured. "I was just so afraid he would be killed." She described Ashley as a "pitiful young boy who has had a nonviolent mental disturbance since he was a child."

The carnival manager later admitted Ashley told him he was one of the FBI's Most Wanted fugitives. But the manager said he did not believe him.

No. 214
DUANE EARL POPE

First Most Wanted Listing:
June 11, 1965
Apprehended:
June 11, 1965

A college football hero and clarinetist in the school band, Duane Pope made the Most Wanted List in 1965 for what was called "the modern era's bloodiest bank robbery."

Pope, who had graduated from McPherson (Kansas) College with a degree in industrial arts only a week previously, walked into a Big Springs, Nebraska, bank on June 4, 1965. He talked to employees about a loan, then pulled a silencer-equipped .22 caliber automatic and forced four employees to lie face down on the floor. He shot all four people and robbed the bank of $1,598. Though seriously wounded, one employee survived and sounded the alarm.

The break in the robbery came when a policeman on the beat in Salina, Kansas, found a rental car in town that was identified as the one used in the crime, about 400 miles away. Pope had used his own name in renting the automobile.

A nationwide search was mounted for Pope, whom the FBI described as a "brawny campus athlete and gun enthusiast." The release went on to say that Pope was known "as an accomplished athlete and was co-captain of the football team at McPherson College."

On the day he was named to the Most Wanted List, Pope responded to an appeal from McPherson's president, Desmond Bittinger, that he give himself up. Pope called Bittinger and said, "I heard your plea for me to give myself up, and I decided this is the thing to do. I am going to turn myself in."

Pope then called police in Kansas City, Missouri, who picked him up in a city hotel. "I'm tired of running, come and get me," he was quoted as saying to police.

Pope was charged with the murder of the seventy-seven-year-old bank president, Andreas Kjeldgaard, a fifty-nine year old cashier, Glen Hendricks, and a thirty-five-year-old bookkeeper, Lois Ann Hothan. The twenty-five-year-old assistant cashier who had turned in the alarm testified at the trial from a wheelchair.

Pope was sentenced to death, but he was spared when the US Supreme Court vacated the sentence on a legal technicality in 1970. He was then prosecuted by the state of Nebraska on a murder charge and sentenced to life in prison.

No. 220
EDWARD OWEN WATKINS

First Most Wanted Listing:
September 21, 1965
Apprehended:
December 2, 1965

Here is the FBI's announcement from "The FBI" television program of November 7, 1965:

This is Assistant Director C. D. DeLoach speaking to you from FBI Headquarters in Washington. On behalf of FBI Director J. Edgar Hoover, I would like to thank the American public for their splendid support in helping combat crime and subversion.

Only through such wholehearted cooperation can the security of our nation be maintained.

Today, a new reign of lawlessness threatens us, typified by one of the FBI's current "Ten Most Wanted Fugitives." You may now be in possession of information that would aid in his location.

He is Edward Owen Watkins, a convicted armed robber, now charged with robbing a series of Ohio banks of over $103,000 this year. A forty-six-year-old American, Watkins is 5 feet 10 inches tall, weighs about 190 pounds, has black, graying hair, brown eyes and a heavy build. Believed heavily armed with revolvers, Watkins is probably accompanied by a twenty-two-year-old striptease dancer and model, Kathleen Marie Rosen, also wanted for a bank robbery violation. She is 5 feet 6 inches tall, 118 pounds, medium build and tanned complexion. Her dark brown hair may be dyed.

Watkins is extremely dangerous and no private citizen should attempt to apprehend him. Please report any information concerning him or Rosen to the nearest FBI office.

Now, please join us in viewing tonight's episode of "The FBI."

No. 221
JOEL SINGER

First Most Wanted Listing:
November 19, 1965
Apprehended:
December 1, 1965

The use of a 20mm Finnish antitank gun in the robbery of a Brink's vault in Syracuse, New York, set off a nationwide furor over the easy availability of heavy weapons and turned Joel Singer, a Canadian native, into an international fugitive.

Singer was charged with the $423,421 burglary of a Brink's armored vault in the morning hours of October 24, 1965. The FBI said that Singer and accomplices were allegedly equipped with drills, cutting torches, electronic devices, gas masks, dynamite, nitroglycerin, mattresses, and blankets. They used the gun to break through the vault's eighteen-inch-thick walls.

Authorities later said that the weapon was bought in Alexandria, Virginia, by men later reported to the FBI as being "suspicious." The gun was shipped to Plattsburgh, New York, and later to Montreal, Canada. The Royal Canadian Mounted Police kept a daily surveillance of the warehouse in which it was stored, but the gun was removed at night by the thieves.

On October 30, 1965, FBI agents, aided by the navy and coast guard, recovered the antitank gun from the waters near Jones Beach, New York, and it was identified as the weapon used in the robbery.

The next day, Singer's uncle, Jack Frank, was arrested by FBI agents in Garden City, New York, on conspiracy charges. Warrants issued on October 29 and November 1 charged Singer with violation of the Federal Firearms Act and conspiracy to cause the interstate transportation of stolen property.

A statement issued by the FBI said: "Joel Singer, charged in a spectacular $423,000 Brink's burglary in Syracuse, New York, in October, 1965, was arrested on December 1st in Montreal, Canada, following an intensive joint investigation by FBI and Canadian authorities."

The case caused at least one newspaper to editorialize against the ease with which the criminals obtained the cannon. The *Milwaukee Journal* wrote: "The 20 mm. cannon used by burglars to blast their way into a Brink's vault in Syracuse may have been stolen, but the point isn't too important. The burglars, who got away with an estimated $400,000, could just as easily have ordered the weapon over the counter or by mail from any one of a number of firearm dealers.

"It remains incredible that such weapons of mass destruction are so readily available in this easygoing nation."

No. 231
JIMMY LEWIS PARKER

First Most Wanted Listing:
February 25, 1966
Apprehended:
March 4, 1966

The FBI description on the release naming escapee Jimmy Parker to the Most Wanted List left a vivid picture. Parker had been imprisoned for the gunshot slaying of his estranged wife's parents but escaped from a prison bus by sawing through the bars on the rear doors.

The release read: "A white American, born in Iredell County, North Carolina, on April 24, 1935, he is 5'11" tall, weighs 148 pounds, has a slender build, ruddy complexion, blue eyes and brown hair which may be dyed blond or red. Tattooed on his left arm are dice and the name 'June.' The name 'Jim' is tattooed on his right arm. He reportedly keeps constant company with women, drinks large amounts of milk for stomach ulcers, smokes cigars and cigarettes, drinks beer and whiskey, likes television, is skilled at pencil sketching and plays the guitar poorly."

Parker was arrested in Detroit, Michigan, where he was living under an alias.

No. 233
ROBERT CLAYTON BUICK

First Most Wanted Listing:
March 24, 1966
Apprehended:
March 29, 1966

In another era Robert Buick might have been called daring, perhaps even dashing.

Born in Pennsylvania, he spent much of his life in Mexico and even took up the sport of bullfighting. At the same time, however, Buick was also making a living robbing California banks. In 1966, he was named to the Most Wanted List, accused of robbing eighteen federally insured savings and loan associations in that area, some of them twice.

Buick was nearly brought down in February 1966 when a retired police officer, unaware Buick had just robbed a bank but suspicious of his actions, pursued him several miles before overtaking him for questioning. When the former officer attempted to detain Buick, he was bitten on the hand. The escapee sped away in his Buick station wagon.

The FBI release gave this description of the fugitive:

> Said to be a personal "playboy type" extrovert who likes attention and the opportunity to boast of his past bullfighting activity, Buick reportedly drinks expensive wines and liquors, frequents good restaurants, nightclubs and beach resorts and likes swimming, boating, dancing, television and jazz music. He is known to dress neatly and conservatively, to travel by air and private automobile, usually exceeding the speed limit, and to wear a diamond ring, a gold identification wrist bracelet and a gold religious neck medal. Buick reportedly smokes cigarettes, is es-

pecially fond of Italian and Mexican food and is fairly fluent in the Spanish language.

Buick offered no resistance when he was arrested by local authorities in Pecos, Texas.

No. 234
JAMES VERNON TAYLOR

First Most Wanted Listing:
April 4, 1966
Apprehended:
April 4, 1966

On April 4, 1966, just a few hours after James Taylor was added to the Most Wanted List, fingerprints from a previously unknown body found floating April 1 in the harbor at Baltimore, Maryland, were identified as Taylor's.

The former mental patient, who was accused of the mutilation and slaying of his wife and three young children, was presumed to have drowned.

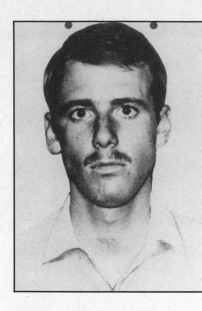

No. 236
JAMES ROBERT RINGROSE

First Most Wanted Listing:
April 15, 1966
Apprehended:
March 29, 1967

While Mexico and Canada have often been used as havens for FBI fugitives, James Ringrose put more distance between himself and US authorities. Unfortunately for Ringrose, his habit of writing bad checks was discovered in Japan. Japanese authorities arrested him and, despite his denials, identified him through his fingerprints appearing on an FBI Most Wanted notice.

Ringrose had been added to the Most Wanted List after he and accomplices were accused of passing fraudulent checks worth hundreds of thousands of dollars throughout the United States, utilizing fictitious bank accounts opened under assumed names, and counterfeit cashier's checks that were exchanged for easily cashed traveler's checks.

When asked by Japanese authorities why he was writing bad checks, Ringrose replied, "Why not? Banks are insured and insurance companies are making huge profits. So who's getting hurt? I am helping retailers by spending the money."

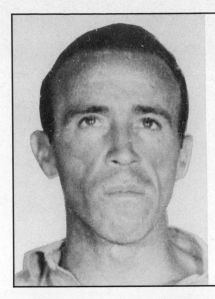

No. 241
GENE ROBERT JENNINGS

First Most Wanted Listing:
December 15, 1966
Apprehended:
February 14, 1967

A kidnaper and prison escapee, Gene Jennings went to great lengths to change his appearance to throw authorities off the track. But just short of having spent two months on the Most Wanted List, Jennings was arrested in an Atlantic City, New Jersey, apartment, living under the name of Joseph Cook. He had attempted to disguise himself by increasing his height with extra stockings in his shoes and by covering an identifiable tattoo with tape.

No. 243
MONROE HICKSON

First Most Wanted Listing:
February 17, 1967
Apprehended:
January 30, 1968

When the FBI called Monroe Hickson "mean, ruthless, intelligent and cunning," you can bet they were not exaggerating. Hickson joined the Most Wanted List after his escape from the Manning Correctional Institution in Columbia, South Carolina, on March 10, 1966.

At the time, Hickson was serving four consecutive life sentences for murder that were imposed in 1957. In 1946, while carrying out robberies, Hickson murdered four store proprietors in Aiken, South Carolina, killing one man with an ax, one woman with a club, and a husband and wife with pistol shots.

He was also convicted and sentenced to two consecutive twenty-year terms for two cases of assault and battery with intent to kill resulting from brutal attacks with bricks on two female storekeepers.

Hickson's case was closed on January 30, 1968, when the fingerprints of a man who had died at Chapel Hill, North Carolina, were identified as Hickson's.

No. 251
DONALD RICHARD BUSSMEYER

First Most Wanted Listing:
June 28, 1967
Apprehended:
August 24, 1967

Is there honor among thieves? Not according to Donald Bussmeyer.

The FBI's search for this fugitive uncovered a great deal of information about the "hulking and heavily tattooed alleged bank robber," including the fact that he once robbed a bank of $75,000 with two accomplices, then took $45,000 as his share, leaving two "disgruntled" compatriots.

Bussmeyer, who had served a thirteen-year term for robbery, was also sought by Los Angeles police on a dozen charges of robbery and kidnaping that were related to a series of local department store holdups.

The FBI's physical description of the fugitive said: "His numerous tattoos include 'Easy to Hate,' 'Don,' a boy, a heart with an arrow, 'Mom,' a sailboat and a cross on his right arm. An ace of hearts, an ace of spades, a cross, a bird, 'Cool Man,' a dagger, a ship, two dice, 'Born,' 'Win,' 'Joyce,' a star and a tiger are tattooed on his left arm. On the back of his left hand he has the tattoos 'Born to Win' and a set of dice. On his chest he bears the tattoos 'Don Bussmeyer Loves Joyce,' a heart, 'Rum,' and 'Coke.' Tattoos of a woman appear on each shoulder blade."

Bussmeyer was said to be accompanied by his wife, whom the FBI said was constantly armed with one or more weapons and was reported to be an excellent shot. "She reportedly often practices by shooting out the flame on candles," the FBI said.

The FBI caught up with Bussmeyer as he slept in an Upland, California, apartment. Also arrested were his wife and another man, who was charged with harboring a fugitive.

No. 252
FLORENCIO LOPEZ MATIONG

First Most Wanted Listing:
July 1, 1967
Apprehended:
July 16, 1967

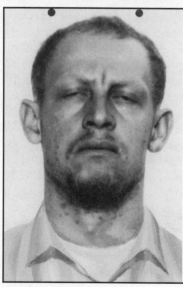

No. 253
VICTOR JERALD BONO

First Most Wanted Listing:
July 1, 1967
Apprehended:
July 16, 1967

When tear gas flooded the Los Angeles apartment on July 16, 1967, Florencio Mationg and Victor Bono, still heavily armed, were forced to give themselves up to FBI agents. The pair, along with two others, had been sought in the brutal murder of two border patrol officers.

The two uniformed inspectors of the Immigration and Naturalization Service Border Patrol had disappeared from their Southern California highway checkpoint on June 16, 1967. They were found in a remote mountain cabin near Anza, California, two days later, handcuffed together around an old stove. Both had been shot in the head.

An FBI search of Bono's Perris, California, residence later located a large arsenal of weapons—including seven rifles, four shotguns, three submachine guns, a pistol, and thousands of rounds of ammunition—plus a 400-pound cache of marijuana valued at the time at $150,000. Mationg had previously been convicted of robbery, possession of narcotics, kidnaping, and escape; and Bono, of possession of narcotics.

The pair were captured just weeks after making the List when the FBI raided their Los Angeles apartment. After they did not emerge, tear gas was fired, and Mationg surrendered peacefully. Bono resisted briefly but was subdued, according to the FBI. Five revolvers and a machine gun were later found in the apartment.

No. 254
ALFRED JOHNSON COOPER, JR.

First Most Wanted Listing:
July 27, 1967
Apprehended:
September 8, 1967

Citizen cooperation has played a large role in the capture of many of the FBI's Most Wanted, with many criminals brought to justice after their pictures were recognized in newspapers or on television.

Alfred Cooper, Jr.'s, picture was also recognized—not in the media, but by a visitor on a tour of FBI headquarters. Cooper had been sought by the FBI for unlawful interstate flight to avoid prosecution for robbery, assault and battery of a law enforcement officer, and also for kidnaping.

Cooper and two accomplices allegedly robbed a gas station and engaged in a vicious gun battle with a local policeman, who was shot several times, losing the sight in one eye.

A little over a month after Cooper was placed on the Most Wanted List, the FBI released this statement: "Cooper was seized by FBI agents on Friday afternoon, September 8, on a downtown Boston street corner. He was using the alias Joe Brady and his location was directly aided by a visitor to FBI headquarters in Washington, D.C., who recently viewed his photograph on the FBI tour route and furnished valuable information."

No. 261
JERRY REECE PEACOCK

First Most Wanted Listing:
December 14, 1967
Apprehended:
March 5, 1968

In the annals of prison escapes, Jerry Peacock rates at least a footnote. Imprisoned in the California State Prison at Soledad, on October 23, 1966, Peacock and an accomplice scaled a fence with a stolen ladder after binding and gagging a boiler-room custodian. They then completed the escape by leaping aboard a slow-moving potato truck on a nearby highway.

Peacock, originally sentenced to prison after robbing a fellow armored car driver in Santa Ana, California, followed up the escape with a robbery, a kidnaping, and a murder charge. He reportedly beat a man to death in Hollywood.

Less than three months after being added to the Most Wanted List, he was arrested by FBI agents at a ranch near Mesquite, Nevada, where he was working under an alias as a hired hand. According to the FBI, he had grown a beard and lost considerable weight in an attempt to conceal his identity.

No. 262
RONALD EUGENE STORCK

First Most Wanted Listing:
January 19, 1968
Apprehended:
February 29, 1968

Just months after being paroled from prison, Ronald Storck was suspected of having shot to death three members of a Pennsylvania family, including an eleven-year-old. Three months later, Storck was apparently readying himself for a long trip on a recently purchased thirty-foot boat.

But the FBI caught up to Storck in the Honolulu, Hawaii, boat harbor and arrested him before he was able to use the two pistols and rifle found aboard the sailing vessel.

No. 264
WILLIAM GARRIN ALLEN II

First Most Wanted Listing:
February 9, 1968
Apprehended:
March 23, 1968

No. 265
CHARLES LEE HERRON

First Most Wanted Listing:
February 9, 1968
Apprehended:
June 18, 1986

The typical criminal named to the Most Wanted List lasts 157 days before being apprehended. Charles Herron was hardly typical.

Sought by the FBI along with Herron after two police officers were murdered in Nashville, Tennessee, on January 16, 1968, William Allen II was apprehended by FBI agents in Brooklyn, New York, just weeks after he was named to the List on February 9, 1968. The two Tennessee officers had attempted to stop a car allegedly occupied by Herron, Allen, and two others when they were cut down by shots from a high-powered rifle. One officer was killed instantly by a .30-30 bullet in the chest and the other died sixty days later.

In 1974, however, Allen escaped from the Tennessee Penitentiary where he was serving a ninety-nine-year sentence for the slaying. Herron remained free, only to have his freedom jeopardized when Allen made what proved to be a small but fatal mistake.

In 1986, Allen attempted to renew a falsified driver's license in Jacksonville, Florida. A suspicious examiner summoned state troopers, who found that Allen had at least three sets of identification. Allen refused to identify himself, so troopers went to his home to learn more about him. There they found Herron.

At the time of the arrest, William H. Webster, then director of the FBI, said, "Herron's apprehension demonstrates the effectiveness of our law enforcement system and the doggedness of its personnel. Because an examiner in the Division of Motor Vehicles did her job, the Florida Highway Patrol and the Jacksonville Sheriff's Office were able to uncover the faint trail which led our Agents to one of our country's most elusive fugitives. Cooperation among agencies and the determination within them are the keys to this success."

Herron's stay on the Most Wanted List finally ended after eighteen years, four months, and nine days.

No. 268
JOHN CONWAY PATTERSON

First Most Wanted Listing:
February 26, 1968
Apprehended:
March 17, 1968

Police from Milwaukee, Wisconsin, took John Patterson into custody March 17, 1968, in what must have seemed to them an average arrest at the time. Only later did they found out Patterson was wanted for the murder of an East St. Louis, Illinois, police officer and the wounding of another during the robbery of a liquor store.

Patterson and an accomplice reportedly entered the liquor store wielding revolvers and demanding money from the cash register. When the proprietor sounded the burglar alarm, the robbers stuffed the loot in their pockets and tried to escape through the front door. Confronted by two police officers responding to the robbery alarm, the gunmen seized the two store owners and used them as shields in the ensuing gun battle. One officer was mortally wounded, the other seriously.

Patterson reportedly escaped in a getaway car parked nearby, while his accomplice was quickly apprehended.

In Milwaukee a tactical police squad reported they saw a suspicious man standing between two buildings in the early morning hours. When the squad pulled up, Patterson jumped into an automobile and fled at high speed. He was curbed a short while later and arrested without further incident.

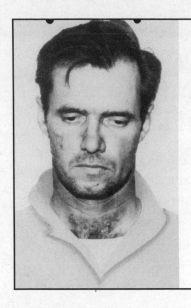

No. 275
FRANKLIN ALLEN PARIS

First Most Wanted Listing:
April 9, 1968
Apprehended:
May 21, 1968

Franklin Paris joined the Most Wanted List when he failed to appear for a hearing after being arrested for a supermarket burglary. California authorities also charged Paris with committing a series of masked robberies and kidnapings in which he forced store managers to provide money from their safes while holding members of their families as hostages.

The FBI said that Paris was a skilled burglar and had reportedly been taught by a close relative how to commit burglaries and crack safes.

Paris was eventually captured at Lakehead, California, following a running gun battle with FBI agents and California police. During the gun fight, Paris was wounded three times, and a large arsenal of weapons, including rifles, pistols, bayonets, a shotgun, and gas masks, was recovered from his car.

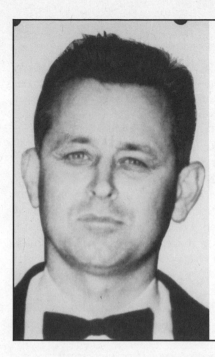

No. 277 and No. 351
JAMES EARL RAY

First Most Wanted Listing:
April 20, 1968
Apprehended:
June 8, 1968

Second Most Wanted Listing:
June 11, 1977
Apprehended:
June 13, 1977

James Earl Ray had always wanted to be on the Most Wanted List. He was granted that request on April 20, 1968, when he was named as "special addition No. 11" after he assassinated civil rights leader Rev. Dr. Martin Luther King, Jr.

The FBI was able to pinpoint Ray within days of the April 4 murder in Memphis, Tennessee, by identifying fingerprints left on the rifle that was found within a block of the crime scene, and by descriptions from people in the area and at a Memphis motel where Ray had stayed.

The FBI bulletin said the Bureau had ordered the special addition of Ray "to insure the widest possible dissemination of Ray's photograph and description to help effect his earlier possible location."

The FBI said Ray had an arrest record dating back to 1949. He had been convicted of burglary, armed robbery, and forging US Postal Money Orders, and had been confined in the Los Angeles County Jail; the Joliet and Pontiac, Illinois, state prisons; and the US Penitentiary at Leavenworth, Kansas. He had served in the army between February 1946 and December 1948, received a three-month sentence at hard labor for being drunk and breaking arrest, and was given a General Discharge due to "ineptness and lack of adaptability for military service."

Ray was also sought for his escape from the Missouri State Penitentiary, on April 23, 1967, where he had been serving a twenty-year sentence following convictions for armed robbery and operating a motor vehicle without permission of the owner.

Ray's capture came with international help. After the murder the fugitive made his way to Canada, where he had spent time previously. In Canada he obtained a passport under the name of Ramon George Sneyd. He flew from Toronto to London, and after a few days he flew from London to Portugal, then back to London. On June 8, 1968, Ray again packed his bags, this time planning to travel by airplane to Brussels. But British authorities intercepted and arrested him, tipped off that Sneyd was actually Ray.

After returning to the United States, Ray proclaimed his innocence, then changed his mind and pleaded guilty. He was sentenced to ninety-nine years in prison. The trial did nothing to squelch talk of a possible conspiracy in the murder, however, and Ray later even took issue with his own attorney by saying he did not agree with the notion there had not been a conspiracy. Among the reasons for the conspiracy theory were Ray's ineptness as a criminal and the fact that he had no evident emotional reason for killing King.

Ray himself pointed to a shadowy figure named Raoul who gave him thousands of dollars and who, Ray said, may have set him up for the murder.

Ray made the Most Wanted List a second time after escaping from the Brushy Mountain Prison in Tennessee on his third attempt. He and six other inmates were involved in the escape, but one was shot off the prison wall. Fifty-four hours later, Ray was recaptured in a wooded area of the Cumberland Mountains, only five miles from the prison.

In 1981, Ray again made national headlines when he was stabbed twenty-two times by fellow inmates. He recovered from the wounds, which needed seventy-seven stitches to be closed.

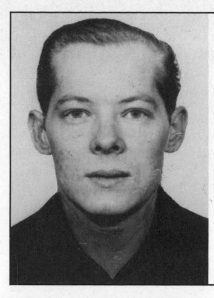

No. 290
RICHARD LEE TINGLER

First Most Wanted Listing:
December 20, 1968
Apprehended:
May 19, 1969

The last customer in the Columbus, Ohio, dairy store on the evening of October 20, 1968, probably never even made the three employees—the female store manager, a fifteen-year-old boy, and an eighteen-year-old girl —look twice.

But the customer pulled a gun and ordered the girl to lock the door. He then bound them hand and foot and gagged them, after taking just over $500 from the till. But rather than leave, Tingler turned toward the employees, severely beat the teenagers about the head, then shot them in the back of the head with a pistol. The woman manager was severely beaten, and strangled with a wire coat hanger, but she survived to identify a mug shot of Richard Tingler.

Based on the autopsies and in particular the bullets found in the bodies, Columbus, Ohio, police also issued warrants in connection with four murders in that city in September 1968. In the early morning of September 16, the bodies of three men and a woman had been found in a Cleveland park, each shot in the head, some several times. The group was said to be a local tavern owner, two employees, and a local woman.

Tingler had previously been convicted of eleven counts of breaking and entering in Ohio in May 1961 and was imprisoned for three years. He was imprisoned again for a parole violation from January 1965 to February 1968 before again being placed on parole.

The FBI bulletin also said that Tingler had reportedly dressed as a woman, and sketches were sent out portraying the fugitive in female clothes and a female hairdo.

After Tingler was named to the Most Wanted List, his photograph was shown on the television program "The FBI" in March 1969. Two months later, the FBI was contacted by local authorities in Washita County, Oklahoma, who requested help in checking out someone they suspected might be wanted by the Bureau.

A farmer said that his newly hired hand was acting peculiar. When shown a photo of Tingler, the farmer identified him as his hand, Don Williams. Despite being armed, Tingler gave up without a struggle. He was sentenced to death, but his sentence was commuted to life in prison on death row.

No. 292
GARY STEVEN KRIST

First Most Wanted Listing:
December 20, 1968
Apprehended:
December 22, 1968

No. 293
RUTH EISEMANN-SCHIER

First Most Wanted Listing:
December 28, 1968
Apprehended:
March 5, 1969

Ruth Eisemann-Schier was the first woman to make the Most Wanted List. Eisemann-Schier and her boyfriend Gary Krist were sought by the FBI for perpetrating one of the most sensational crimes in the List's history. On December 17, 1968, they abducted Barbara Jane Mackle, the twenty-year-old daughter of a Coral Gables, Florida, real estate developer, and buried her alive for eighty hours, until ransom arrangements were made.

Mackle was abducted from an Atlanta motel room, where Krist and

Eisemann-Schier tied up Mackle's mother and then forced Mackle to accompany them. She was taken to a spot deep in the Georgia woods where a grave was waiting. She was placed in a box equipped with a battery, a fan to circulate air through two flexible vent pipes that would protrude just above the ground, and a small supply of food and water—and buried under eighteen inches of dirt.

Shortly afterward, her parents were contacted and given instructions on how to proceed to pay the ransom for their daughter's safe return. The kidnapers' ransom note also told of their daughter's condition and said if the Mackles attempted to have authorities intervene, they would never find out where Barbara was buried and she would eventually suffocate.

The kidnapers asked for $500,000, with rigid conditions. The money was to consist of recently issued $20 bills, none older than 1950 issues, no more than ten notes to have consecutive serial numbers; there was to be no form of marking on the bills. The Mackles were also told to purchase a classified ad in the personal section of a paper in their Miami hometown.

When the money was collected and the personal ad placed, the Mackles—with FBI assistance—made their first attempt to drop off a suitcase filled with the money. But signals were switched. The money was picked up, but not by the kidnapers. The Miami police, who were not aware of the plan, scared off a stranger, who dropped a suitcase. In it was the ransom.

The kidnapers called and accused the Mackles of missing the drop-off. But they were given another chance with a new drop-off spot. This time, the money was picked up. Shortly thereafter, the FBI's office in Atlanta was given directions to a buried capsule. There, Barbara Mackle was found—eighty hours after first being buried alive. Although ten pounds lighter, she was remarkably calm and composed.

While the kidnaping was still in progress, the FBI had begun to piece together clues that led them to Gary Krist, working at the University of Miami Marine Institute as a research technician under the alias of George Deacon, and to Ruth Eisemann-Schier, a Honduran native and a graduate student at the same institute.

On December 20, even before Mackle was safe, Director J. Edgar Hoover, who became personally involved in the case, announced that kidnaping warrants were issued for Krist, twenty-three at the time, and Eisemann-Schier, who was twenty-six. Soon after, the pair joined the Most Wanted List. The trail heated up the same night, when a car rented to George Deacon was found at West Palm Beach. A local boat dealer said that he had sold a boat that day to a man named Arthur Horowitz, who paid $2,300 in denominations of $20 from a suitcase crammed with money.

The FBI traced the boat through forms signed at navigation locks across Florida. Agents in helicopters and planes recognized Krist and his boat when he moved into the Gulf from Fort Myers. With helicopters in pursuit,

Krist swung north into Charlotte Harbor and beached his speedboat at Hog Island—a swamp- and jungle-covered island, three miles long and a half-mile wide, inhabited only by alligators, rattlesnakes, and mosquitoes.

Agents and local police on foot eventually closed in on Krist and arrested him. In the rotting hull of a boat on the island, the FBI found almost half of the half-million-dollar ransom.

Eisemann-Schier, however, remained loose, and in the next weeks, stories in newspapers around the country told of the "unknown factor" in the spectacular kidnaping. Described as "not bad looking" by one fellow worker, she was considered friendly, considerate, and slightly coquettish by those who knew her.

She was finally arrested in Norman, Oklahoma, where she was working as a carhop at a drive-in restaurant. Her fingerprints had been identified after she had applied for a job as a nurse at a state hospital in Norman.

A fellow employee said that she had introduced the fugitive to her son. "She didn't seem to drink or carouse," the woman said. "There are a lot of girls I wouldn't introduce to my son. I am shocked."

Krist, it was later reported, was an escapee from a California prison, where he'd been serving a term for theft of a vehicle and a prior prison escape. He was accompanied by another inmate, who was killed by a guard as he and Krist were going over a security fence.

Krist was given a life prison term but was paroled after ten years. Eisemann-Schier, meanwhile, pleaded guilty and was given a seven-year term, but she was paroled in 1972 and ordered deported to the Honduras.

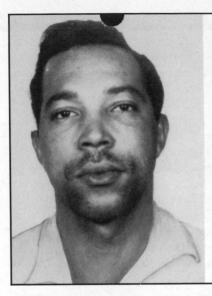

No. 295
BILLIE AUSTIN BRYANT

First Most Wanted Listing:
**January 8, 1969
(approximately 5 P.M.)**
Apprehended:
**January 8, 1969
(approximately 7 P.M.)**

The shortest stay on the Most Wanted List—two hours—was also among the costliest of the Bureau's additions. Billie Austin Bryant was added to the List after he killed two FBI agents who were attempting to arrest him following a bank robbery in which he was a suspect.

The FBI's search for Bryant actually began in August 1968, when Bryant, who was serving an eighteen- to fifty-four-year term for robbery and assault, escaped from the District of Columbia Department of Corrections Reformatory at Lorton, Virginia, by reportedly crashing a prison vehicle through a chain-link gate.

In the following months agents for the FBI tracked Bryant. Among the individuals the Bureau watched for leads was Bryant's estranged wife, who lived in Washington, D.C.

Three agents, twenty-six-year-old Anthony Palmisano, twenty-seven-year-old Edwin Woodriffe, and frequent partner George Sullivan, decided to check on her after a bank in Prince Georges County, Maryland, was robbed of $1,700 on Wednesday morning, January 8. Bryant had been identified by a teller who remembered him as a former customer.

Newspaper stories after the incident said that the three agents went to the door of Bryant's wife's apartment and knocked. Someone opened the door, the stories said, and shot down Woodriffe and Palmisano, and then slammed it. Sullivan, who was out of the line of fire, reportedly fired two shots into the closed door and then ran to his car to radio for help. While he was gone, the gunman apparently escaped.

When Sullivan identified Bryant as the man who shot the agents, Bryant was named as a "special addition" to the Most Wanted List, and hundreds of agents and Washington, D.C., police began an intensive manhunt in the area of the shooting.

Two hours later, a nearby apartment tenant, who had been watching televised news reports of the slayings, summoned the police after his dog called attention to mysterious noises in the attic by whining and barking restlessly.

Charles Monroe, a police captain who was called to the scene, admitted he was "a little frightened" when he pointed a shotgun toward the attic entrance, located in a hall, and called out: "Is anybody up there?"

"Yes, I'm up here," came the reply. "I'm Billie Austin Bryant."

Described as meek and mud-covered, Bryant dropped out his pistol through the door and surrendered without resisting.

Found guilty of the two murders, Bryant—described as unrepentant—was sentenced to two consecutive life terms rather than the death penalty. That, the judge said, would deny him "the luxury of all the special attention a capital penalty would generate."

Before his sentencing, Bryant said, "I can't say I'm sorry for what happened to the two men. I feel they brought their death on their own self. To stand here and say I'm sorry would be a lie. I had a job to do, and I did it. If killing men means surviving, I'm afraid I'd have to do it over."

The judge further described Bryant as "Escape motivated, incorrigible and extremely dangerous. He can only be controlled in an institution like Atlanta or Leavenworth.

"The capital penalty, if imposed, would keep him here indefinitely in the death cell of our antiquated jail. Several years might pass while various appeals and hearings ran their course. If a new trial became necessary because of new legal doctrine relating to the capital penalty no one can tell whether essential witnesses would be available."

Palmisano and Woodriffe were the twenty-second and twenty-third FBI agents to be killed in the line of duty. Woodriffe died of a gunshot to the brain, Palmisano of massive hemorrhaging in his chest. Palmisano was married with no children. Woodriffe, the first black agent killed in the line of duty, was married with two young children.

No. 300
CAMERON DAVID BISHOP

First Most Wanted Listing:
April 15, 1969
Apprehended:
March 12, 1975

Cameron Bishop was a man just a few months ahead of his time. Bishop, named to the List on April 15, 1969, is generally considered to be the first of the 1970s radicals and revolutionaries to make the Most Wanted List.

Bishop's FBI release read: "Cameron David Bishop, a violence-minded college revolutionary who bears the tattoo of a skunk and is charged with sabotage in the dynamiting of Colorado power transmission towers, has been added to the FBI's list of Ten Most Wanted Fugitives."

Bishop was only the second individual in United States history charged under the 1918 Sabotage Act, which made destroying power lines during a time of national emergency a federal offense.

At the time of the bombings, Bishop was free on bond awaiting trial for participating in a sit-in demonstration at Colorado State University during which demonstrators seized the third floor of a college classroom building. Charges of second-degree burglary and conspiracy to commit burglary were later filed against several demonstrators, including Bishop, whom the FBI said was "reputedly an active member of the Students for a Democratic Society, a loudly militant New Left group opposed to US involvement in Vietnam and existing government policies."

At the time, police said that the bombings were apparently in protest against the Vietnam War, since the power company lines served plants manufacturing defense materials.

Bishop was arrested in East Greenwich, Rhode Island, six years after being named to the List. His automobile contained what authorities said was a small arsenal of weapons.

Arrested along with Bishop was Raymond Levasseur, who later would end up being named to the List as fugitive number 350. A police officer said the two had apparently been casing a bank and that an anonymous phone call had reported suspicious men in an automobile in the bank's parking lot. "They had all kinds of weapons and enough ammunition to start their own war."

Bishop was found guilty later that year of violation of the Sabotage Act and sentenced to seven years in prison, but the United States Circuit Court of Appeals in Denver overturned the conviction in 1977, saying Bishop could not have known of the 1918 law.

No. 301
MARIE DEAN ARRINGTON

First Most Wanted Listing:
May 29, 1969
Apprehended:
December 22, 1971

It took nearly twenty years for the first woman to be named to the Most Wanted List. It took only a matter of months for the second woman to achieve this position.

Marie Arrington was added to the Most Wanted List after she escaped from the Florida Correctional Institution for Women at Lowell, Florida. On March 1, 1969, she cut through a heavy window screen and either scaled two tall barbed-wire-topped fences or slipped under a double-locked gate. Arrington was awaiting execution after conviction for murdering a Florida secretary, a crime she committed while free on appeal bond following a conviction for killing her former husband.

After riddling the secretary with bullets, Arrington reportedly ran over her several times with an automobile, possibly in revenge against the secretary's superior, who, as public defender, had unsuccessfully defended two of Arrington's children on felony charges.

The FBI flyer on Arrington described her as a smooth-talking "confidence" woman and expert forger, "who dresses neatly in colorful clothes, frequents nightclubs, drinks alcoholic beverages heavily and chain smokes cigarettes."

Arrington was arrested by FBI agents in New Orleans, where she was employed under the name Lola Nero.

The 1960s
Rogues' Gallery

No. 124
KENNETH RAY LAWSON

First Most Wanted Listing:
January 4, 1960
Apprehended:
March 20, 1960

Wanted after a daring escape from the Tennessee State Penitentiary in Nashville on April 22, 1959.

No. 125
TED JACOB RINEHART

First Most Wanted Listing:
January 25, 1960
Apprehended:
March 6, 1960

Rinehart, who once allegedly boasted he would "make 'Baby Face' Nelson look like a piker," had been imprisoned for armed robbery and was sought as a parole violator.

No. 139
ROBERT WILLIAM SCHULTZ, JR.

First Most Wanted Listing:
October 12, 1960
Apprehended:
November 4, 1960

The FBI release on Schultz said that he was a "revenge-crazed, jail-hardened bank robber and prison escapee" who had "allegedly threatened the lives of a United States Marshal, a Federal Judge and a former accomplice."

No. 140
MERLE LYLE GALL

First Most Wanted Listing:
October 17, 1960
Apprehended:
January 18, 1961

Gall, who was said to hate law enforcement officers and reportedly claimed he would not die happy unless he killed one, failed to appear for his incarceration after a conviction on charges of burglary. He was wanted for unlawful flight.

No. 141
JAMES GEORGE ECONOMOU

First Most Wanted Listing:
October 31, 1960
Apprehended:
March 22, 1961

On August 23, 1958, while Economou was serving a California robbery sentence and working with fellow prisoners in a remote forest area, he became involved in a violent fight with another inmate and guarding officers. After being subdued and handcuffed and while awaiting removal to more secure confinement, Economou broke loose, forded a nearby creek, and disappeared into the thick underbrush. He completed his escape, managing to file off his handcuffs, and was added to the Most Wanted List when he allegedly fled California.

No. 144
HERBERT HOOVER HUFFMAN

First Most Wanted Listing:
December 19, 1960
Apprehended:
December 29, 1960

Huffman, a truck driver, allegedly sent $100 by wire to his common-law wife in North Carolina, with instructions for her to meet him in Chicago. There, he reportedly told an acquaintance of his insane jealousy and his belief that the woman had been unfaithful to him, saying that he would teach the woman a lesson. The two were known to have registered in a Chicago hotel. The next morning, hotel employees were summoned to a room to check on a report of a "sick" woman. In the room they discovered the nude body of Huffman's wife, brutally beaten and burned in various places, apparently from a cigarette and a torch made from a roll of paper.

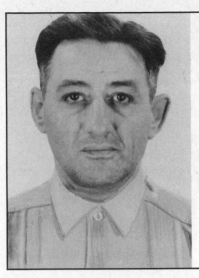

No. 146
THOMAS VIOLA

First Most Wanted Listing:
January 17, 1961
Apprehended:
March 27, 1961

After being sentenced to a life term for the gangland-style slaying of a Warren, Ohio, steak-house owner and his nephew in 1941, Viola escaped from the Ohio Penitentiary at Columbus in 1960. A citizen recognized Viola's photograph in an issue of *This Week* magazine, and he was captured in a Detroit apartment. "The minute I knew the FBI had put me on the 'Top Ten,' I knew my free time was up and those men would get me," said Viola after his arrest.

No. 149
WILLIAM TERRY NICHOLS

First Most Wanted Listing:
April 6, 1961
Apprehended:
April 30, 1962

Considered an "incorrigible" inmate, Nichols escaped from a Seminole

County, Georgia, work gang after seizing a guard's shotgun and pistol and locking the officer in a prison truck. He was serving a sentence for robbery but had previously been convicted of armed robbery, burglary, grand larceny, and transporting illegal whiskey. He had also made several jail breaks from Alabama and Georgia prisons.

No. 152
KENNETH HOLLECK SHARP

First Most Wanted Listing:
May 1, 1961
Apprehended:
July 3, 1961

After he forfeited a bond for his release on charges of larceny, Sharp was allegedly the trigger man in the murder of a seventy-five-year-old Chicago man during the holdup of a Chicago service station on September 11, 1952.

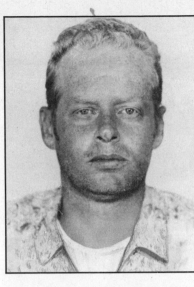

No. 155
ROBERT WILLIAM SCHUETTE

First Most Wanted Listing:
July 19, 1961
Apprehended:
August 2, 1961

Schuette, serving a twenty-year sentence for armed robbery, escaped from the Maryland State Penitentiary in Baltimore in October 1961. Over the next ten months, Schuette said that he hid out in Maine, Florida, Texas, California, and finally in Chicago, where he said he had changed his address forty different times and held twenty to twenty-five jobs in order to avoid arrest.

No. 156
CHESTER ANDERSON MCGONIGAL

First Most Wanted Listing:
August 14, 1961
Apprehended:
August 17, 1961

Wanted for interstate flight to avoid prosecution for attempted murder,

McGonigal had already been convicted of assault with intent to kill, felonious assault, burglary, and larceny.

No. 159
JOHN ROBERT SAWYER

First Most Wanted Listing:
October 31, 1961
Apprehended:
November 3, 1961

Wanted for a vicious bank robbery in which an Omaha, Nebraska, bank manager and his wife were held hostage overnight and in which Sawyer and an accomplice allegedly stole $72,599. The bank manager was viciously pistol-whipped by the bandits during the incident.

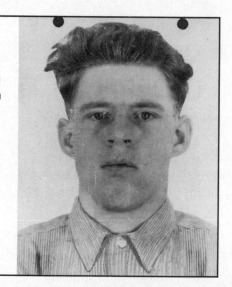

No. 161
FRANKLIN EUGENE ALLTOP

First Most Wanted Listing:
November 22, 1961
Apprehended:
February 2, 1962

When released on parole in 1959 from a prison sentence of one to twenty-five years for a 1954 shotgun robbery in Ohio, Alltop was immediately taken into custody by West Virginia authorities to stand trial for another shotgun holdup in 1954. While awaiting trial in West Virginia, Alltop and three cellmates escaped by sawing through bars on a second-floor cell and lowering themselves to the ground with blankets they'd tied together.

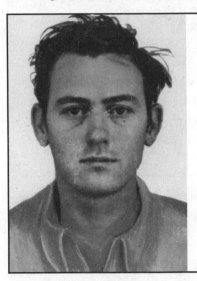

No. 163
DELBERT HENRY LINAWEAVER

First Most Wanted Listing:
January 30, 1962
Apprehended:
February 5, 1962

While awaiting transfer to the State Penitentiary at Lansing, Kansas, to serve a five- to ten-year burglary sentence, Linaweaver escaped from a Salina, Kansas, jail, brutally beating two officers on the head with a sack of broken glass.

No. 172
JOHN KINCHLOE DEJARNETTE

First Most Wanted Listing:
November 30, 1962
Apprehended:
December 3, 1962

The FBI described DeJarnette as a "fast-moving, veteran gunman, narcotics user and Federal parole violator" and sought him after three alleged bank robberies in Kentucky and Ohio. The Bureau said DeJarnette may have been traveling with a twenty-eight-year-old woman wanted on federal charges of interstate flight to avoid prosecution for obtaining narcotics by fraud and deceit and that DeJarnette had used explosives to escape from prison.

No. 176
JERRY CLARENCE RUSH

First Most Wanted Listing:
January 14, 1963
Apprehended:
March 25, 1963

The FBI release on Rush said: "Jerry Clarence Rush, a trigger-happy, shotgun-toting alleged bank robber, tattooed with the words 'Born to lose' and believed using bank robbery loot to finance a big-spending honeymoon with his stripteaser bride, is one of the FBI's 'Ten Most Wanted Fugitives.' "

No. 177
MARSHALL FRANK CHRISMAN

First Most Wanted Listing:
February 7, 1963
Apprehended:
May 21, 1963

Chrisman was named to the Most Wanted List after robbing a Toledo, Ohio, bank of $12,264.

No. 180
CARL CLOSE

First Most Wanted Listing:
September 25, 1963
Apprehended:
September 26, 1963

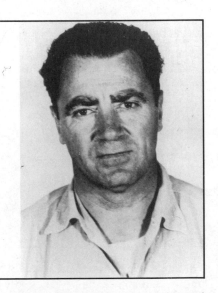

On parole after serving twelve years for bank robbery, Close was charged with committing another pair of bank jobs in Maryland and Virginia.

No. 182
ALFRED OPONOWICZ

First Most Wanted Listing:
November 27, 1963
Apprehended:
December 23, 1964

Arrested while fleeing from an attempted burglary of a Cleveland Trust Company branch building, Oponowicz departed during a recess of his trial, leaving his wife holding his hat and coat in the courtroom.

No. 184
JESSE JAMES
GILBERT

First Most Wanted Listing:
January 27, 1964
Apprehended:
February 26, 1964

Gilbert escaped from California's San Quentin Prison on June 20, 1963, and he and an accomplice allegedly robbed a savings and loan in Alhambra, California, of $11,500 on January 3, 1964. Using a female employee as a shield, Gilbert allegedly shot and killed an Alhambra police sergeant with a

.45 caliber automatic during his flight. Police officers shot the second bank robber.

No. 186
FRANK B. DUMONT

First Most Wanted Listing:
March 10, 1964
Apprehended:
April 27, 1964

Convicted six times for crimes related to burglary and wanted on charges of fleeing to avoid prosecution for aggravated assault on a fourteen-year-old girl, Dumont was captured in Tucson, Arizona, by a barefoot police officer and a former college wrestler. Dumont was seen rifling through an apartment by the manager, who alerted two tenants, one of whom was an off-duty police officer. The officer raced after Dumont barefoot and caught him. He was joined by a former Notre Dame wrestler, who applied a hammerlock on Dumont until authorities arrived.

No. 187
WILLIAM BEVERLY HUGHES

First Most Wanted Listing:
March 18, 1964
Apprehended:
April 11, 1964

While serving a twenty-year sentence after pleading guilty to robbing an Alabama beverage sales company at gunpoint, Hughes escaped from prison and fled in a state-owned truck. Hughes, who had been dishonorably discharged from the US Army, had previously been convicted of transporting a stolen motor vehicle interstate, burglary, larceny, and armed robbery, and court-martialed for theft of government property, carrying a concealed weapon, and attempted desertion.

No. 194
EDWARD NEWTON NIVENS

First Most Wanted Listing:
May 28, 1964
Apprehended:
June 2, 1964

Released only two months previously after convictions on charges of armed robbery, forgery, and interstate transportation of a stolen vehicle, Nivens walked into a Toledo, Ohio, bar and seized $375, then shot a customer and commandeered a car driven by a passing motorist.

No. 196
THOMAS EDWARD GALLOWAY

First Most Wanted Listing:
June 24, 1964
Apprehended:
July 17, 1964

The FBI bulletin on Galloway read: "Thomas Edward Galloway, a woman-beater with a high I.Q., who lives luxuriously off the earnings of prostitutes and is charged with the gunshot murder of a St. Louis underworld figure. . . ."

No. 202
NORMAN BELYEA GORHAM

First Most Wanted Listing:
December 10, 1964
Apprehended:
May 27, 1965

Alleged Massachusetts bank robber Gorham, living under an alias in a Los Angeles apartment, was seized by FBI agents and local police.

No. 210
DONALD DEAN RAINEY

First Most Wanted Listing:
March 26, 1965
Apprehended:
June 22, 1965

Rainey was charged with bank robbery after he and his sixteen-year-old son allegedly robbed a Del Rey, California, bank—while Rainey was on conditional release from a federal penitentiary for robbing the same bank eight years previously.

No. 216
THEODORE MATTHEW BRECHTEL

First Most Wanted Listing:
June 30, 1965
Apprehended:
August 16, 1965

Wanted for interstate flight to avoid prosecution for armed robbery, Brechtel was seized in Chicago at his place of employment, where he was working as a painter. Although he had been using an alias, he admitted his identity to arresting agents and stated, "I know what you want. I'm it."

No. 218
WARREN CLEVELAND OSBORNE

First Most Wanted Listing:
August 12, 1965
Apprehended:
September 9, 1965

Pursuing his estranged wife into a Nashville, Tennessee, beauty parlor, Osborne allegedly shot and killed the proprietor before threatening to kill his wife.

No. 219
HOLICE PAUL BLACK

First Most Wanted Listing:
August 25, 1965
Apprehended:
December 15, 1965

Black was wanted for the murder of a Chicago policeman. After the murder Black moved to Miami and took a job. He grew a mustache and a goatee and wore dark glasses and a cap in an attempt to change his appearance from the clean-shaven look of his Most Wanted poster. With the help of a tip from a citizen, he was seized by FBI agents outside his "cheap rooming house," according to a newspaper story. "He wasn't expecting it—none of them are," said an arresting FBI agent. "He was quite surprised that we had found him."

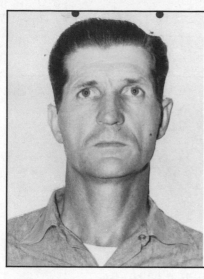

No. 225
JAMES ROBERT BISHOP

First Most Wanted Listing:
January 10, 1966
Apprehended:
January 21, 1966

Bishop, who boasted that he had passed bogus checks worth thousands of dollars all over the United States, was wanted after fleeing to avoid prosecution on an armed robbery charge.

No. 229
CHARLES LORIN GOVE

First Most Wanted Listing:
February 16, 1966
Apprehended:
February 16, 1966

With fellow Most Wanted List mate Robert Dwayne Owen, Gove escaped from the California Medical Facility at Vacaville, California, on October 31, 1965. The pair allegedly first ransacked a California ranch, then robbed a Kentucky bank of $6,800 on November 23, 1965, returning less than a month later to take another $14,500 from the same bank. Gove was apprehended on the same day he was added to the Most Wanted List. He was spotted by FBI agents among a throng of Mardi Gras celebrants on Bourbon Street in New Orleans.

No. 232
JACK DANIELS SAYADOFF

First Most Wanted Listing:
March 17, 1966
Apprehended:
March 24, 1966

Wanted for bank robbery, kidnaping, and interstate transportation of a stolen vehicle, Sayadoff had been charged with holdups in Illinois, California, and Ohio.

No. 235
LYNWOOD IRWIN MEARES

First Most Wanted Listing:
April 11, 1966
Apprehended:
May 2, 1967

Meares had a career criminal record spanning thirty-five years. He escaped from a North Carolina prison while serving sentences for breaking and entering, larceny, and storebreaking. Meares's criminal career, which began in 1931, also included convictions for bank burglary, housebreaking, receiving stolen goods, grand larceny, automobile larceny, and escape. An expert safecracker, he called himself the Old Master.

No. 237
WALTER LEONARD LESCZYNSKI

First Most Wanted Listing:
June 16, 1966
Apprehended:
September 9, 1966

Wanted for bank robbery, Lesczynski had previously been convicted of bank robbery, armed robbery, and petty larceny. The FBI bulletin noted the fugitive's distinguishing scars and marks included several bullet wounds on his body.

No. 238
DONALD ROGER SMELLEY

First Most Wanted Listing:
June 30, 1966
Apprehended:
November 7, 1966

Smelley failed to appear in court in Albuquerque, New Mexico, to face trial on two charges of armed robbery of the same supermarket in February and March 1964. During the second robbery he allegedly shot at a store employee while leaving the site. He was arrested by FBI agents in a Hollywood, California, bar and grill. He told arresting agents, "I'm glad it's over. You guys are too hot for me."

No. 239
GEORGE BEN EDMONDSON

First Most Wanted Listing:
September 21, 1966
Apprehended:
June 28, 1967

Edmondson, who was said to have a high IQ and to have become a skilled computer operator while taking data processing courses while incarcerated, escaped from prison in Missouri after being convicted on charges of armed robbery.

No. 242
CLARENCE WILBERT MCFARLAND

First Most Wanted Listing:
December 22, 1966
Apprehended:
April 4, 1967

Imprisoned after an armed robbery of a Washington, D.C., bank and a gunshot-filled automobile chase, McFarland escaped from a Rockville, Maryland, prison. He reportedly used a cell bar that had been sawed loose to pry open a heavy wire window screen, gaining access to an adjacent exercise yard. He then scaled a twelve-foot-high jail wall and completed his escape.

No. 244
CLYDE EDWARD
LAWS

First Most Wanted Listing:
February 28, 1967
Apprehended:
May 18, 1967

Laws and an accomplice allegedly robbed a Wheaton, Maryland, supermarket of some $1,500 and, while fleeing in Laws's car, were stopped by two police officers, one of whom Laws shot in the stomach. Laws was reportedly shot in the leg in the return fire but still managed to flee.

No. 247
THOMAS FRANKLIN
DORMAN

First Most Wanted Listing:
April 20, 1967
Apprehended:
May 20, 1967

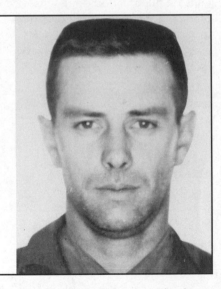

The FBI release on Dorman read: "Thomas Franklin Dorman, who bears the tattoo 'Born to Lose' on his left arm and is charged with kidnaping a motorist following a gun battle with Maryland police, as he and an accomplice allegedly fled from an armed robbery, has been added to the FBI's list." During the gunfight with Maryland police, one officer was seriously wounded in the stomach.

No. 255
JOHN D. SLATON

First Most Wanted Listing:
August 2, 1967
Apprehended:
December 1, 1967

After police in Oroville, Washington, attempted to question him about a bad check, Slaton fled in his car and, when cornered in a trailer where he was camping, shot an officer and escaped on foot.

No. 270
GEORGE BENJAMIN WILLIAMS

First Most Wanted Listing:
March 18, 1968
Apprehended:
June 19, 1968

Williams, who spent most of his adult life in prison, was sought by the FBI after allegedly robbing in 1965 the same California bank he had victimized in 1946. Williams, described as a "loner" and a "river rat," began his criminal career in 1931 and had been convicted of bank robbery, grand larceny, possessing counterfeit coins, and escape.

No. 271
MICHAEL JOHN SANDERS

First Most Wanted Listing:
March 21, 1968
Apprehended:
April 8, 1968

Wanted for armed robbery, Sanders and three accomplices allegedly overpowered two Santa Cruz County, California, deputy sheriffs while being questioned for loitering. They disarmed the officers and fled in a waiting car, firing a parting shot toward the officers. An amateur karate fan, according to the FBI, Sanders was apprehended in New York City, where he was living under an alias and teaching karate.

No. 283
ROBERT LEROY LINDBLAD

First Most Wanted Listing:
July 11, 1968
Apprehended:
October 7, 1968

Lindblad, described as a well-armed judo and karate expert, was sought in connection with the gunshot murders of two heavily insured businessmen, whose bodies were found in a shallow grave near Dayton, Nevada. A surviving partner and two others were later charged with conspiracy in the murders and arrested; Lindblad was named as the alleged gun for hire.

No. 296
BILLY LEN SCHALES

First Most Wanted Listing:
January 27, 1969
Apprehended:
January 30, 1969

With a long history of sex offenses, Schales was added to the Most Wanted List after allegedly contacting a Houston, Texas, housewife at her home in order to inspect an apartment advertised for rent. After luring her to the apartment, Schales allegedly attacked the woman and, during a furious struggle, stabbed her repeatedly in the neck with a knife.

No. 297
THOMAS JAMES LUCAS

First Most Wanted Listing:
February 13, 1969
Apprehended:
February 26, 1969

A suspect in a series of Maryland bank robberies along with a gang of eleven others, Lucas was charged after allegedly participating in the $22,398 robbery of a Baltimore bank.

No. 298
WARREN DAVID REDDOCK

First Most Wanted Listing:
March 11, 1969
Apprehended:
April 14, 1971

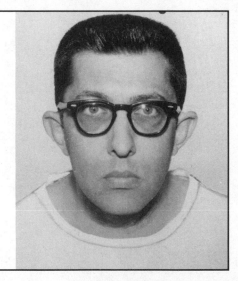

A paroled forger who was charged with the murder of an Illinois business associate, Reddock was apprehended by FBI agents at Pacifica, California, where he was employed under an assumed name at a ranch and kennel.

No. 299
GEORGE EDWARD BLUE

First Most Wanted Listing:
March 20, 1969
Apprehended:
March 28, 1969

Less than a month after his release from prison on probation, Blue allegedly participated in the robbery at gunpoint of an Evansville, Indiana, bank. He was described by the FBI as a weight lifter who patronized health food and vitamin stores.

No. 303
FRANCIS LEROY HOHIMER

First Most Wanted Listing:
June 20, 1969
Apprehended:
December 20, 1969

Arrested after a $57,000 robbery of a Denver philanthropist, Hohimer was detained in Alton, Illinois, but was released on a $25,000 bond and fled. His FBI report said that tattoos on Hohimer's right arm included the initials KH and HK, the names Katherine and Sherry, and symbols of a scroll, a horseshoe, four aces, a heart, flower, leaves, and blossoms.

The 1970s

Introduction

The Vietnam War was thousands of miles away, but its echo was heard loudly throughout the United States. The Most Wanted List was no exception to the mood of the 1970s.

Only months into the new decade, the FBI made the single largest addition to the Most Wanted List to date—four "political revolutionaries" who were suspected of being involved in the bombing of a US Army math research center at the University of Wisconsin, Madison. A researcher was killed in that incident.

Another month after this lengthy addition to the List, the Bureau named three more Most Wanted revolutionaries, bringing the Most Wanted List to a total of sixteen fugitives, the highest number ever listed to date.

At that time, although the FBI stated that the capture of these radicals was its highest priority, two of the sixteen were never captured and were later removed from the Most Wanted List.

Bernardine Rae Dohrn, fugitive number 314, was typical of the "revolutionaries." Raised in an upper-class suburb of Milwaukee, Wisconsin, Dohrn had received Bachelor of Arts, Master of Arts, and Doctor of Law degrees from the prestigious University of Chicago—yet she was sought by the FBI on a long list of charges.

Years later, the FBI admitted that it had had trouble with apprehending the political fugitives because they did not fit the patterning of the typical criminal. "They have a tendency to go underground," an FBI spokesman said in 1983. "They have the moral stamina to cut themselves off completely from family and friends, something many criminals won't do."

No. 307
LAWRENCE ROBERT PLAMONDON

First Most Wanted Listing:
May 5, 1970
Apprehended:
July 23, 1970

The addition of Lawrence "Pun" Plamondon to the Most Wanted List made him a hero to the underground movement that had begun to grow in the United States during the early 1970s. It also made him a worried man.

"I'm not going to be apprehended," Plamondon boasted in one newspaper story. But he was definitely concerned, according to the writer, who knew him. "The press release that the FBI is sending out about me being a crazed criminal is just setting it up so they can be justified in killing me when they find me."

The FBI release called Plamondon the reputed "Minister of Defense" of the revolutionary "White Panther Party" and said he had been charged with the dynamite bombing of a Central Intelligence Agency office in Chicago.

The bulletin went on:

> The "White Panther Party" has been publicly described as a "hippie" group which supports the Black Panther Party and advocates revolution in the United States. Plamondon has reportedly been active in a "hippie" commune known as "Trans-Love Energies" in Ann Arbor, Michigan, said to be a source of narcotics traffic. He is also known to closely associate with "hard rock bands" and underground newspapers throughout the country and is reportedly a regular user of marijuana, hashish and drugs such as LSD.
>
> Acquaintances describe his normal appearance as dirty and

unkempt and his living, eating and hygienic habits as poor. He reportedly usually dressed in "hippie" style, but may adopt neater dressing habits to evade capture. He is said to enjoy living in a communal manner and to have a pronounced persecution complex.

Plamondon reportedly possesses a rifle and shotgun, has allegedly used dynamite in a crime for which he is sought and should be considered very dangerous.

The FBI's bulletin proved to be a font of information for law enforcement officials. Plamondon was finally arrested 250 days after first making the List. On his way in a Volkswagen bus from New York to the Upper Peninsula of Michigan, Plamondon was stopped by a state trooper for littering. The trooper let the van go with a warning after looking at the identification cards of Plamondon's two companions and a set of fake papers Plamondon was carrying.

A story in the *Milwaukee Journal* at the time told the rest:

> Then in a fateful, ironic twist, the state trooper listened to a bulletin flashed over a national police network that Plamondon had been seen earlier in the day in Pontiac, 200 miles further south. The irony was that the report was a false alarm, one of many that police had unsuccessfully checked out.
>
> But the trooper radioed a report ahead that he had stopped a van with "two suspicious looking hippies and another guy." He gave the St. Ignace state police post their names. A check turned up Forrest as one of Plamondon's co-defendants, and the search was on.
>
> In a matter of minutes, the two police cars converged on the van as it was riding steadily along US 2, west of the bridge.
>
> Plamondon was carrying a loaded derringer and there was a loaded rifle in the van, but he put up no resistance.

When arrested, Plamondon had only a grizzled growth of beard and moderately short hair.

No. 308
HUBERT GEROID BROWN

First Most Wanted Listing:
May 6, 1970
Apprehended:
October 16, 1971

The Most Wanted List usually shines the spotlight of notoriety on a little-known fugitive. That was not the case with H. "Rap" Brown.

By the time Brown became a "special addition" to the Most Wanted List as the number eleven fugitive, he had already been arrested once by the FBI, charged with inciting a riot after making a speech in Cambridge, Maryland. After the forty-five-minute speech 1,000 blacks rioted for two hours, and a fire spread along two city blocks, destroying about a dozen buildings as volunteer firemen refused to enter the district and extinguish the blaze.

Brown, chairman of the Student Nonviolent Co-ordinating Committee, had also been indicted in Louisiana on charges of assaulting a federal officer and found guilty of violating the Federal Firearms Act.

In March 1970 Brown was named a Most Wanted fugitive after he failed to appear in Ellicott City, Maryland, for his trial on the riot charge. A federal warrant was issued charging Brown with unlawful interstate flight to avoid prosecution.

FBI agents arrested Brown two days later in Washington, D.C. As he was brought into a US courthouse by agents, he told newsmen, "We'll burn the country down, honkies and all."

The Bureau went after Brown again when he failed to appear for his trial after legal moves led to a change in venue. Brown obtained expert legal help but did not show up for the start of his trial. Rumors at the time suggested he feared an attempt on his life and had gone into hiding.

Named to the Most Wanted List on May 6, 1970, he was said to have been in the United States "alive and carrying out revolutionary activity," according to Eldridge Cleaver, the then-exiled Black Panther.

He was finally arrested following a gun battle with New York police in October 1971. Brown was among four men arrested in connection with a shooting that occurred outside a bar after a holdup. In the running gunfight that followed, Brown received a bullet wound in the abdomen, and a policeman was wounded. Brown drew a five- to fifteen-year sentence for the crime.

In 1983, Brown, who had since changed his name to Jamil Abdullah al-Amin, said that he disavowed the violence that he had previously advocated and was living according to Islamic law.

No. 309
ANGELA YVONNE DAVIS

First Most Wanted Listing:
August 18, 1970
Apprehended:
October 13, 1970

The FBI's reluctance to place women on the Most Wanted List ended with the revolutionary era of the 1970s. Nowhere was this more evident than when Angela Davis, a former university philosophy instructor, was named a Most Wanted fugitive.

Educated at Brandeis University, Davis was an avowed communist, whose upbringing in the Deep South in the 1960s had made a strong impression on her. The FBI began their search for Davis days after an abortive attempt, led by Jonathan Peter Jackson, to free three San Quentin convicts from custody at the Marin County, California, Courthouse. Five hostages were taken by the convicts and Jackson, including Superior Court Judge Harold J. Haley, who was killed. In the shoot-out with police officials which resulted, two of the convicts and Jackson were killed and the third convict was wounded. An assistant district attorney was wounded, as was one of three women jurors also held hostage.

While Davis was not seen anywhere near the shootout, she was accused of purchasing the weapons used in the breakout attempt and charged under a California law that makes an accomplice equally guilty. The FBI began the search when a federal charge of interstate flight to avoid murder and kidnaping charges were leveled against her.

The FBI description of Davis read: "A Negro American, Davis was born on January 26, 1944, in Birmingham, Alabama. She is five feet eight inches tall, weighs 140 pounds, has brown eyes, brown hair and a thin build. She has a brown complexion and occasionally wears 'granny-type' glasses. She styles her hair in a natural 'Afro' fashion and has been known by the nickname 'Tamu.' "

Davis eluded the FBI for nearly two months, but when a planned flight to Cuba fell through, agents were able to pick up her trail. Her arrest, in a mid-Manhattan motel, was personally announced by Attorney General John Mitchell.

Davis was returned to California for a trial two years later but found not guilty of all charges by an all-white jury. The verdict was greeted by loud applause from a supportive audience, which also gave the jurors a great round of applause as they filed out.

In an autobiography she wrote two years after her acquittal, Davis said that she had spent the two months hiding "underground" with the help of friends.

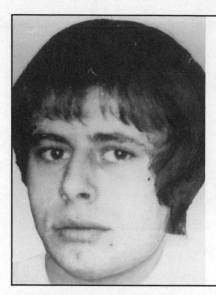

No. 310
DWIGHT ALAN ARMSTRONG

First Most Wanted Listing:
September 4, 1970
Removed:
April 7, 1976

No. 311
KARLETON LEWIS ARMSTRONG

First Most Wanted Listing:
September 4, 1970
Apprehended:
February 16, 1972

Less than four months after National Guardsmen at Kent State University in Ohio killed four students, the climactic incident in a series of violent actions took place on the campus of the University of Wisconsin, Madison.

On August 24, 1970, a van loaded with a homemade bomb exploded next to Sterling Hall in Madison, killing one person, injuring three more,

No. 312
DAVID SYLVAN FINE

First Most Wanted Listing:
September 4, 1970
Apprehended:
January 8, 1976

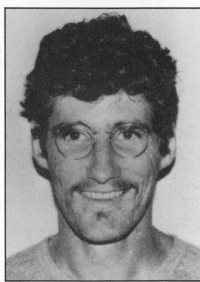

No. 313
LEO FREDERICK BURT

First Most Wanted Listing:
September 4, 1970
Removed:
April 7, 1976

and gutting the building, which housed the Army Mathematics Research Center.

Government officials responded rapidly. The Wisconsin attorney general said, "We've got the beginnings here of an outright revolution."

J. Edgar Hoover made a rare public appearance on network television and added four suspects to the Most Wanted List: Dwight Alan Armstrong,

Karleton Lewis Armstrong, David Sylvan Fine, and Leo Frederick Burt. Yet despite one of the largest FBI manhunts in history, the agency has never caught all four of these fugitives.

The bombing was actually one of a series by members of the group called the New Year's Gang, after an abortive attempt to bomb a Wisconsin ammunition plant from an airplane on New Year's Eve, 1969. Three bombs dropped harmlessly on the facility, which shipped rockets to American forces in Vietnam.

Another bombing on the Madison campus caused only $900 in damage to an ROTC classroom building. Another incident, however, inflicted $60,000 in damage on an ROTC facility.

Interviews with the subjects years later showed that planning for the fatal bombing began three weeks prior to the August 24 blast. Karleton Armstrong later explained the target's significance. "Army Math was always the ultimate target in Madison. For two years, ever since its relationship to secret projects like the electronic battlefield and the air war in Vietnam was exposed, every demonstration was directed at removing Army Math."

Makings of the bomb included fifty-five-gallon drums, forty-six gallons of fuel oil, seven hundred pounds of fertilizer, dynamite, caps, and fuses. The material was loaded into a stolen van, which was placed next to the hall on a weekend—a time when, as shown by the gang's previous surveillance, no one typically was in the facility. The blast, which broke windows for blocks around, opened a hole in the six-story building and collapsed interior walls.

This time, the hall was not vacant. After the blast, one graduate student was found buried alive, saved by a door frame. Another postdoctoral student walked away in a state of shock, with only cuts and bruises. A security officer was also pulled out alive.

But Robert Fassnacht, a thirty-three-year-old postdoctoral physics researcher with a wife and three children, was found dead underwater in the basement. He was a victim, it was theorized, of concussive effects of the blast.

Karleton Armstrong was the first of the group to be arrested, eighteen months later, under the alias of David Weller, by the Royal Canadian Mounted Police in Toronto. He was returned to Wisconsin and convicted on several counts in connection with the death. He served eight years of a fourteen-year sentence.

David Fine was arrested January 7, 1976, in San Rafael, California, and was sentenced to seven years in prison. He served only three years.

Both Dwight Armstrong and Leo Burt were removed from the Most Wanted List on April 7, 1976, but shortly afterward, Armstrong was arrested in Canada and was sentenced to seven years in prison. He served three years. He was paroled but then received a five-year prison term in 1988 in Indiana on charges of conspiracy to distribute methamphetamine.

Burt remains at large.

No. 314
BERNARDINE RAE DOHRN

First Most Wanted Listing:
October 14, 1970
Process Dismissed:
December 7, 1973

At five feet five inches and 125 pounds, with a Doctor of Law degree, Bernardine Dohrn would hardly have seemed the type to have made the Most Wanted List. But during the turmoil of the late 1960s and early 1970s, Dohrn's activities drew attention from authorities who named her in these five major federal indictments: interstate flight to avoid prosecution for mob action; antiriot law; bombing matter; unlawful possession or receipt of firearms; and conspiracy.

Dohrn had originally been indicted in Chicago, where she had taken part in a series of violent demonstrations that the FBI said were sponsored by the militant Weatherman group. On October 9, 1969, a women's group of the Weatherman faction held a demonstration resulting in a violent confrontation with Chicago police and Dohrn's subsequent arrest and indictment. When she failed to appear for her trial, the federal government began a series of indictments and an intensive search. Dohrn became the fourth woman to be added to the Most Wanted List.

The FBI's bulletin listing said that Dohrn had allegedly sent communications to major newspapers condemning United States policies and urging violent revolution and guerrilla warfare to overthrow American society. The communications included threats to commit widespread bombings and assaults.

Dohrn, who earned her undergraduate and graduate degrees at the University of Chicago, "reportedly may resist arrest," according to the FBI, which also said she "has been associated with persons who advocate the use of explosives, and she may have acquired firearms. She should be considered very dangerous."

Dorhn was dropped from the Most Wanted List in December 1973, when the bomb conspiracy charges against her were dismissed. The dismissal came in federal court in Detroit, when the government said it could not disclose details of its electronic surveillance in the case without jeopardizing national security.

Charges were also dismissed against fourteen other people that same day. All fifteen, including Dohrn, had been charged with conspiring to carry out bombings across the United States at a Flint, Michigan, "war council" in December 1969.

No. 315
KATHERINE ANN POWER

First Most Wanted Listing:
October 17, 1970
Removed:
August 15, 1985

No. 316
SUSAN EDITH SAXE

First Most Wanted Listing:
October 17, 1970
Apprehended:
March 27, 1975

Nineteen years after allegedly participating in a bank robbery during which a Boston police officer was shot and killed, Katherine Ann Power is no longer on the Most Wanted List. Law enforcement authorities would still be most interested in arresting her.

Power and Susan Saxe, both former students at Brandeis University in Waltham, Massachusetts, allegedly joined three Massachusetts parolees in a

September 23, 1970, robbery of the State Street Bank and Trust Company in Boston, during which $26,585 was seized. Shortly after the bank robbers fled with the loot, a Boston police officer—alerted by a silent alarm in the bank—arrived at the crime scene. He was shot and killed in a burst of fire from a semiautomatic .45 caliber Thompson submachine gun.

Saxe allegedly carried a .30 caliber rifle inside the bank during the holdup, and Power drove a getaway car. Both were additionally charged with theft of government property from a National Guard Armory at Newburyport, Massachusetts, on September 20, 1970, and the robbery of a savings and loan in Philadelphia earlier that year.

The FBI said the two women belonged to a "radical, revolutionary group dedicated to attacking the United States military system and undermining police powers."

Five years after she was placed on the List, Saxe was arrested in Philadelphia by police who recognized her from the photo on an FBI flyer. She was unarmed and did not resist arrest. The Bureau said that it had reissued a large number of flyers in the Philadelphia area because it had reason to believe Saxe was in the area.

The FBI said that Power and Saxe had been able to elude authorities because they developed close relationships with people in the women's movement. Several months later, a coalition of women's groups began a protest of what they said was FBI harassment of women. An organizer of the group said the coalition was concerned about FBI tactics during the search for Power and Saxe, and claimed the Bureau was questioning feminist and lesbian leaders in several cities with "utter disregard for the rights of people."

Power was removed from the Most Wanted List in 1984, at which time she was thirty-five years old. The Bureau said it was no longer receiving information about Power. An FBI spokesman said, "She has not been seen since 1974, and we have no indication that she has continued or resumed her criminal activity since her indictment in 1974."

No. 317
MACE BROWN

First Most Wanted Listing:
October 20, 1972
Apprehended:
April 18, 1973

Mace Brown escaped death row once, but he could not outrun the authorities or his death, which came while he was involved in a violent crime.

Brown was added to the Most Wanted List after he participated in a spectacular escape from the District of Columbia Jail on October 2, 1972, while appealing a death sentence.

He had been convicted of first-degree murder of a potential witness in a major narcotics trial. The victim was shot in the head from behind, and Brown received a death sentence.

Brown and seven fellow inmates, three of whom were awaiting trial for murder, broke out of the maximum security section of Washington's century-old jail on a night when many of the inmates were viewing a televised professional football game.

According to the FBI, the escapees cut through steel bars and broke through a metal screen and a glass skylight to reach the jail roof. They then descended to the ground via a fire hose and scaled two twelve-foot-high, barbed-wire-topped fences.

Brown was killed in a gun battle with law enforcement authorities in New York City on April 18, 1973, during an alleged bank robbery attempt.

No. 318
HERMAN BELL

First Most Wanted Listing:
May 9, 1973
Apprehended:
September 2, 1973

In a decade when law enforcement authorities were often targets, Herman Bell was sought as one of their most violent enemies.

Bell was added to the Most Wanted List two years after he was alleged to have participated in the murder of two New York City police officers. The officers, Joseph Piagentini and Waverly Jones, were responding to a call for aid. They were shot outside a Harlem housing complex. An FBI bulletin said the officers were shot several times in the back and that the killers reportedly continued to fire after the victims had fallen.

In addition, Bell and four accomplices were alleged to have robbed a branch of the Bank of America in San Francisco. During the robbery one of the bandits fired a shotgun into the bank vault, injuring a bank employee.

Bell was also sought for questioning in the ambush murders of officers Gregory Foster and Rocco Lauri on Manhattan's Lower East Side on January 27, 1972.

Bell, alleged to have been a "high-echelon officer" in the Black Liberation Army, was arrested on September 2, 1973. He was caught in his car at a New Orleans intersection by FBI agents and local authorities. Local police said they received a tip that Bell was in New Orleans after the arrest of fifteen suspects on multiple charges in San Francisco two weeks previously.

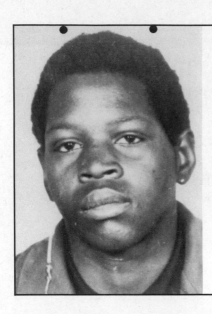

No. 319
TWYMON FORD MYERS

First Most Wanted Listing:
September 28, 1973
Apprehended:
November 14, 1973

The FBI described Twymon Myers as a "violence-prone suspected 'cop killer,' " and his violent end did nothing to dispel the Bureau's description.

The FBI's search for Myers began after a series of crimes, including the robbery of a New York City social club on August 4, 1971. The suspects, who fled the scene in a taxi, engaged pursuing police officers in a shoot-out, resulting in the fatal wounding of the taxi driver.

Meyers was also charged in a complaint filed July 25, 1973, with the robbery of the Bankers Trust Company in the Bronx, New York, on March 16, 1972. The robbers' escape from the bank included an extensive gun battle with pursuing New York City patrolmen.

He was believed to have been involved in the armed robbery of a Queens, New York, savings and loan on April 10, 1973, during which gunshots were fired, and the robbery of yet another bank in the Bronx on July 18, 1973, during which shots were fired from a 9mm automatic.

The FBI said that Myers had reportedly been affiliated with the Black Panther Party and had been "intimately associated with others who have been involved in assaults upon police, killings of police officers, and bank robberies. . . . He allegedly possesses black extremist philosophies and allegedly was a member of the Black Liberation Army, a loosely knit group made up of present and former members of or individuals closely associated with the Black Panther Party."

According to the FBI, Myers was killed in a gun battle with FBI agents and New York City police officers on November 14, 1973, while attempting to resist arrest.

No. 320
RONALD HARVEY

First Most Wanted Listing:
December 7, 1973
Apprehended:
March 27, 1974

No. 321
SAMUEL RICHARD CHRISTIAN

First Most Wanted Listing:
December 7, 1973
Apprehended:
December 11, 1973

The world of professional sports and the Most Wanted List seldom cross paths, but the case of Ronald Harvey and Samuel Richard Christian—a case that had savagery written all over it—involved two of the most famous names in the sports world.

Ronald Harvey and Samuel Christian were allegedly involved in the death of seven individuals in the Washington, D.C., home of basketball player Kareem Abdul-Jabbar and in the murder of a friend of boxing champion Muhammad Ali.

They were reported by the FBI as members of the "Black Mafia," an organization, the FBI said, "which preys upon black communities and deals in murder, narcotics, extortion, the numbers racket and prostitution."

The FBI wrote: "Christian, who is reputed to be a cold-blooded killer and a murderer for pay, is wanted for unlawful flight to avoid prosecution for armed robbery. He has been charged with the wounding of a New York City Police Department detective, and the murder of five individuals resulting from a shoot-out in an Atlantic City, New Jersey, nightclub during a robbery. He allegedly travels with two bodyguards."

Harvey was indicted and charged with participating in the slaying of seven members of the Hanafi American Mussulmans Rifle and Pistol Club in Abdul-Jabbar's home in northwest Washington on January 18, 1973.

The FBI alleged that Harvey and six accomplices, armed with pistols and sawed-off shotguns, entered the headquarters of the Hanafi Mussulmans. "During this slaughter," the FBI wrote, "four children were drowned and in an execution-style manner four adults and a nine-year-old child were shot at close range after they were tied and blindfolded. The nine-year-old and two of the adults were killed; however, the other two adults survived."

Christian was arrested by FBI agents on a street in Detroit on December 11, 1973. According to the FBI, he was given no opportunity to resist.

Harvey was arrested March 27, 1974, but failed to show up for an extradition hearing and forfeited $175,000 bail. He was arrested again in March 1974 in Chicago, and this time bail was set at $3 million.

Harvey was also charged with the shootings of Major B. Coxson—described as a flamboyant entrepreneur, a friend of boxing great Ali, and a Camden, New Jersey, mayoral candidate—and the fifteen-year-old daughter of Coxson's common-law wife.

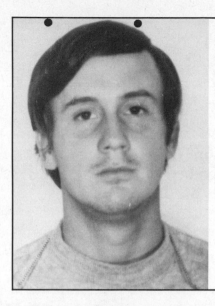

No. 323
LARRY GENE COLE

First Most Wanted Listing:
April 2, 1974
Apprehended:
April 3, 1974

The kidnaping of the wife of a Roanoke, Virginia, businessman was alleged to have been a husband-and-wife job, but only Larry Gene Cole made the Most Wanted List following the crime.

According to the FBI, on March 6, 1974, the victim, a partner in a real estate business, was at a coffee shop near Roanoke when she received a call from a woman who said she was interested in purchasing some property near a resort area. A short time later, the caller met the victim, and they proceeded to drive to the location of the resort property. While en route, the woman told the victim to pull over to the side of the road, and as she did, a car with a single male driver stopped near them. As the driver of the other car approached the victim, she noticed that her passenger was pointing a pistol at her.

A short time later, the husband of the victim received a telephone call demanding $25,000 be paid in small bills for the release of his wife. Early the next morning, the victim was released at an abandoned railroad station at Cotton Hill, West Virginia, after the ransom was paid.

The alleged male kidnaper was named by the FBI as Cole, who was believed to have been accompanied by his wife, Bonnie Ann Cole. He had an extensive criminal record, including convictions for interstate transportation of stolen vehicles, simple burglary, possession of stolen property, and parole violation. His wife had no previous record.

The pair were arrested on April 3, 1974, one day after Cole was named to the List, by New York state police near Buffalo, New York. The FBI reported that the two were unarmed and offered no resistance.

No. 325
LENDELL HUNTER

First Most Wanted Listing:
June 27, 1974
Apprehended:
July 31, 1974

Less than two months after escaping from a Georgia prison camp, the FBI said that Lendell Hunter allegedly broke into a private home in Augusta, Georgia, and beat a seventy-eight-year-old grandmother to death with a grubbing hoe. After slaying the woman, he reportedly assaulted her twelve-year-old grandson, who was sleeping in another room of the house.

Before his escape on December 20, 1972, Hunter was serving three consecutive life prison sentences for rape, in addition to sentences totaling ninety-five years for assault, burglary, and kidnaping.

During the course of one of the rapes, Hunter smashed the victim over the head with an oak table leg, crushing her skull. He then reportedly called the local authorities, using the victim's phone, and hid in the bushes to watch the arrival of local police. As a result of the attack, the victim was blinded in both eyes but regained her sight a year later after brain surgery.

The FBI described Hunter as a loner who had trouble reading but who was found to have an above-average IQ. He allegedly hated women, and while in high school, he reportedly beat female students and a teacher without provocation.

Hunter was apprehended by FBI agents on the street in Des Moines, Iowa, on July 31, 1974. He was unarmed and offered no resistance but denied his identity. Positive identification was made through examination of his fingerprints.

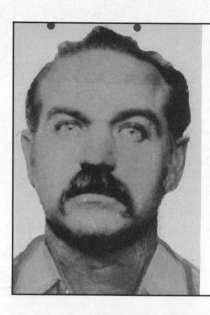

No. 327
MELVIN DALE WALKER

First Most Wanted Listing:
October 16, 1974
Apprehended:
November 9, 1974

From a daring escape to a blazing final chapter, Melvin Walker and a fellow escapee provided headlines for the nation's newspapers in 1974.

On August 10, 1974, Walker and three other prisoners commandeered a garbage truck at gunpoint and rammed their way out of the rear gate of the federal prison near Lewisburg, Pennsylvania. The escaped convicts wasted little time getting back into the swing of their interrupted criminal careers. After abandoning the garbage truck fifteen miles from the prison, they tied up a man and his wife and stole their automobile.

Three days later, the four escapees reportedly robbed a bank at Pollocksville, North Carolina, and escaped with over $16,000. Two of the four escapees were captured following a brief gunfight with lawmen after the bank robbery.

Walker and his remaining fugitive companion, Richard Floyd McCoy, escaped a police dragnet. McCoy had gained national notoriety in 1972 when he hijacked a commercial airliner and bailed out over Provo, Utah, after demanding and receiving over a half-million dollars in ransom. He was arrested two days later and was subsequently sentenced to forty-five years in prison for air piracy.

Walker had escaped from custody on a number of occasions during his criminal career, which dated back to a first conviction for burglary in 1957. He had also been convicted of attempted safe burglary, bank robbery, and escape. During one spree he and a relative were allegedly responsible for five bank robberies, and on another occasion, when he had escaped from custody, he and a fellow escaped convict reportedly committed at least five additional bank robberies.

The FBI said that Walker had engaged in gunfights with police officers to avoid arrest in the past. He had escaped from jail by overpowering his guards and once by using a homemade screw to spread the bars on his prison cell.

Only weeks after their escape, Walker and McCoy were tracked to a quiet neighborhood in Virginia Beach, Virginia. There, the FBI hid for two days until both men left their hideout. The FBI then stationed agents inside and outside the cottage and waited for the two men to return in their car.

An FBI agent was quoted as saying, "McCoy entered the front door with a key, and one of the agents identified himself and told him to hold it right there. The fellow went for his gun and got one shot off, and the agent returned fire." The agent was not injured, but McCoy was killed.

Meanwhile, Walker had not gotten out of the car but was circling the neighborhood. Hearing the gunfire, he took off at a high rate of speed. The car was stopped within a few blocks, and he surrendered peacefully, despite having two loaded weapons in the car.

An arresting agent said, "I think they were using this as one of several pads to cool off. They more or less had gone underground."

No. 328
THOMAS OTIS KNIGHT

First Most Wanted Listing:
December 12, 1974
Apprehended:
December 31, 1974

Held in the cold-blooded slaying of a millionaire Miami industrialist and his wife, Thomas Knight escaped from prison only to be accused in another murder case.

Knight was sought in the double murder of Sydney Gans and his wife on July 17, 1974. After abducting the couple, Knight allegedly drove them to a Miami bank, where he obtained $50,000 in ransom. He subsequently forced them to accompany him to a desolate area of Dade County, Florida.

After reputedly murdering his victims in cold blood, Knight was the subject of a massive manhunt spearheaded by local police and FBI agents, who apprehended him a short time later in the immediate vicinity. He was still in possession of a .30 caliber carbine and the ransom money.

On September 19, 1974, Knight effected his escape—and that of ten other men, all of whom were captured immediately or surrendered—by knocking out a portion of the wall on the second floor of the Dade County Jail. Additionally, Knight and an accomplice allegedly committed an armed robbery of a package liquor store in Cordele, Georgia, on October 21, 1974, during which the two store proprietors were shot in cold blood. One died.

Knight was arrested in an early morning raid on a tenement apartment in New Smyrna Beach, Florida, by FBI agents and local authorities. Although heavily armed, he was said to have offered no resistance.

No. 330
ROBERT GERALD DAVIS

First Most Wanted Listing:
April 4, 1975
Apprehended:
August 5, 1977

Within three days Robert Davis was involved in a pair of crimes that left a thirteen-year-old boy and a police officer dead and many others wounded.

Davis's spree started, according to the FBI, on July 1, 1974, when he and three accomplices allegedly were involved in the $10,000 armed robbery of a Camden, New Jersey, grocery store. During the robbery a thirteen-year-old boy was shot and killed, and five other people were seriously wounded when the bandits and police exchanged gunfire.

On July 3, 1974, two Pittsburgh police officers arrested a man on charges of failure to appear in connection with a narcotics arrest. After the officers handcuffed him, the prisoner broke away and ran to a passing automobile that reportedly contained Davis and another man. As the two policemen approached the car, Davis and his accomplice allegedly opened fire, killing one of the officers.

Davis was arrested without incident by FBI agents on August 5, 1977, in Venice, California.

No. 335
LEONARD PELTIER

First Most Wanted Listing:
December 22, 1975
Apprehended:
February 6, 1976

After the 1960s, FBI bulletins announcing new fugitives to the Most Wanted program rarely showed emotion and were a model of dispassionate, factual writing. The December 22, 1975, announcement that Leonard Peltier had made the list was typical.

There was probably not an FBI agent anywhere who did not want Peltier arrested. The fugitive had been indicted in connection with the shooting deaths of two FBI agents June 26, 1975.

The agents, Ronald Williams and Jack Coler, were involved in a shoot-out on the Pine Ridge Indian Reservation in South Dakota when they attempted to serve a subpoena on a robbery suspect at the reservation. An Indian was also killed in the shootout.

On February 6, 1976, Peltier was arrested by the Royal Canadian Mounted Police near Hinton, Canada. While heavily armed, he offered no resistance.

After receiving a life sentence, Peltier was imprisoned at the Lompoc Federal Prison Camp. He was involved in a prison escape in 1979, in which several inmates were armed, and during which one prisoner died in an exchange of gunfire. Peltier was captured several days later, after a citizen reported that a man fitting Peltier's description had stolen his truck after stealing melons from his yard.

In 1981, Peltier was interviewed from a cell in the federal penitentiary at Marion, Illinois, where he joined the nation's most dangerous and escape-prone convicts, who are housed in individual cells.

While Peltier admitted he was involved in the shoot-out that left the FBI agents dead, he insisted on his innocence. "I never killed nobody, and I don't see why I have to sit here for a life sentence," he said.

"I was raised knowing what your race of people did to mine," he added. "We're at war. We're defending ourselves. I'm sorry those agents died, but I'm also sorry my people died."

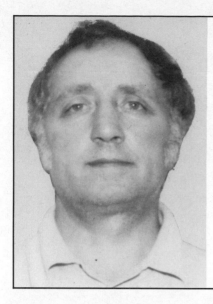

No. 338
ANTHONY MICHAEL JULIANO

First Most Wanted Listing:
March 15, 1976
Apprehended:
March 22, 1976

Many of the FBI's Most Wanted fugitives are hunted down by massive posses of law enforcement officers. Anthony Juliano was caught by a meter maid.

Juliano, who had served twenty-four years in prison for prior bank robbery convictions, was sought in connection with bank robbery conspiracy and as a mandatory release violator from a federal penitentiary. The FBI said he was allegedly part of a pair of bank robbers labeled the "Mutt and Jeff Gang" due to extreme differences in the height of two of the robbers. Juliano, who was five feet two inches tall, was said to have been heavily armed with automatic weapons.

Juliano was recognized by a thirty-five-year-old meter maid in South Hill, Virginia. She notified the sheriff's department, and a deputy, answering the call, saw Juliano driving along a state highway and arrested him.

No. 339
JOSEPH MAURICE MCDONALD

First Most Wanted Listing:
April 1, 1976
Apprehended:
September 15, 1982

When police at Penn Station in New York City arrested a man arriving from Florida, they thought they were making a drug bust.

After he had been held by police for eight hours, the prisoner calmly announced, "Hey, fellas, I'm wanted by the FBI."

That's how Joseph McDonald was apprehended. He had been sought in connection with the theft of $500,000 worth of collector's stamps from a Boston business in 1971. Five years later, a witness scheduled to give testimony against those implicated in the stamp theft was found shot to death.

When arrested, McDonald had $5,000 cash, three silencer-equipped submachine guns, a .45 caliber semiautomatic handgun, and numerous rounds of ammunition in his luggage.

Authorities said they had not ruled out that McDonald, who was sixty-five at the time of his arrest, had links with international terrorism.

No. 343
RICHARD JOSEPH PICARIELLO

First Most Wanted Listing:
July 29, 1976
Apprehended:
October 21, 1976

No. 344
EDWARD PATRICK GULLION, JR.

First Most Wanted Listing:
August 13, 1976
Apprehended:
October 22, 1976

Richard Picariello and Edward Gullion, Jr., both wanted in connection with a series of New England bombings, made the Most Wanted List weeks apart. But they ended their stay only hours apart.

Picariello was named to the Top Ten first. He was charged with interstate transportation of explosive and incendiary devices. The FBI said that Picariello was allegedly a member of a small revolutionary group that obtained funds to finance its operations by robbing banks and purchasing and stealing quantities of explosive devices. The Bureau said he and accomplices were reported to be responsible for bombings in Augusta, Maine; Seabrook, New Hampshire; and the Massachusetts communities of Dorchester, East Boston, and Newburyport.

Gullion, likewise, was sought for interstate transportation of explosives and incendiary devices. His past convictions included robbery, breaking and entering, assault and battery, and narcotics possession.

Picariello was arrested first, in Fall River, Massachusetts. He was said to have resisted arrest and received a minor injury. Gullion was arrested hours later in Providence, Rhode Island.

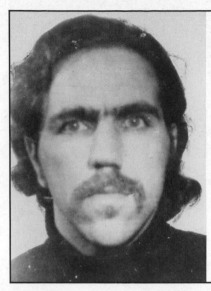

No. 350
RAYMOND LUC LEVASSEUR

First Most Wanted Listing:
May 5, 1977
Apprehended:
November 4, 1984

While the "revolutionary" fervor of the early 1970s began to fade in the middle of the decade, Raymond Levasseur and his friends apparently had a hard time forgetting.

Levasseur was first named to the Most Wanted List on May 5, 1977. He was sought on two federal warrants for bank robbery and unlawful flight to avoid prosecution for unlawful possession of a weapon. At the time, the FBI said that Levasseur reportedly was "a member of a revolutionary group that has claimed credit for several acts of violence" and that he had been known to possess numerous weapons in the past.

Four years later, while still on the Most Wanted List, Levasseur and two other longtime companions were named as suspects in the shooting death of New Jersey state trooper Phillip Lamonaco. The highly decorated trooper apparently stopped an automobile containing Levasseur and several others, including Thomas William Manning, for a routine traffic violation. He was shot eight times in the gun battle that followed. Manning was later named to the Most Wanted List.

Levasseur's eventual arrest included the rare scene of heavily armed FBI agents and local authorities raiding homes in the small farming town of Deerfield, Ohio, an hour south of Cleveland. There, Levasseur and his wife lived about a mile from a post office displaying his photograph and background information. The Levasseurs sent their six- and eight-year-old daughters to a local grade school. Neighbors said that they never suspected the family's past.

School officials said that the children were well behaved, well clothed, well adjusted, attentive to their studies, and respectful of authority. "They were sweet little girls," said one school official. "We're as dumbfounded as everybody else."

The backyard of the Levasseur home included a playground set and a turtle-shaped sandbox bulging with toys. According to neighbors, Levasseur said that he was a sales manager for a cash register company.

In the raids on the homes of Levasseur, Manning, and one other companion, authorities found caches of high-powered rifles and semiautomatic pistols, bomb-making manuals, communiqués of the United Freedom Front—a revolutionary group—about bombings of office buildings in and around New York City, handwritten surveillance notes about two of those corporate targets, and about $32,000 in cash.

Two years later, Levasseur, his wife, Manning, and five others were indicted by a federal grand jury on charges of participating in a nine-year conspiracy of bombings, murder, and bank robbery as members of two political groups. Besides the United Freedom Front, the group was said to have formed the core of the Sam Melville–Jonathan Jackson Unit, which took its name from radicals Jonathan Jackson, shot by police in 1970 in San Rafael, California, and Sam Melville, the alleged ringleader of a Weatherman-affiliated group responsible for the 1969 bombings of eight New York City corporate offices.

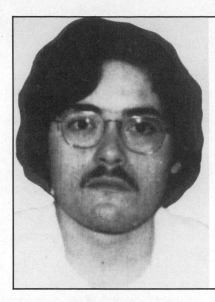

No. 356
CARLOS ALBERTO TORRES

First Most Wanted Listing:
October 19, 1977
Apprehended:
April 4, 1980

A quiet young man, Carlos Alberto Torres was a member of the Episcopal Church's National Commission on Hispanic Affairs and served on its theological task force, helping to write a hymnal and a book of religious texts in Spanish.

Yet, unknown to a good number of his fellow workers, Torres kept a Chicago apartment that police described in April 1977 as a "bomb factory."

At that time, bombs such as those manufactured in Torres's apartment had gone off fifty-eight times in places such as Manhattan; the Chicago Loop; Newark, New Jersey, police headquarters; and Washington, D.C. Most of the bombings were followed by a claim that the blasts were the work of FALN, the Puerto Rican independence organization.

The bomb blasts damaged a number of famous buildings, including the Standard Oil Building in Chicago and Macy's and Bloomingdale's in New York. But they also took a human toll, with four people killed and fifty-five others injured at Fraunces Tavern in New York on January 24, 1975.

Despite a massive investigation, authorities were unable to come up with the identities of any FALN members until a narcotics addict living in the same Chicago apartment building as Torres broke into Torres's apartment. He found 211 sticks of dynamite, walkie-talkies, scores of propane tanks, detonator caps, and various other materials needed to produce bombs. The police arrested the addict when he tried to sell the dynamite, and he led them to Torres's apartment.

After the discovery, police were able to identify as FALN members

Torres; his wife, Haydee Beltran-Torres; Oscar Lopez; and Lucy Rodriguez —all of whom immediately disappeared.

Torres, born in Puerto Rico and raised in Chicago, was named to the Most Wanted List in October 1977, charged with conspiracy and violations of the federal bombing statute, the National Firearms Act, and federal regulations involving explosives.

The Bureau said Torres was believed to have been accompanied by his wife, who had recently been charged with murder by New York State authorities and with a federal bombing-statute violation for her role in one of the incidents for which FALN had claimed credit. The FBI also said that more than sixty actual or attempted bombings had been attributed to the group since October 1974, resulting in five deaths, injuries to over seventy persons, and approximately $5 million in property damages.

Nearly three years later, authorities caught up with Torres, and they may have foiled another terrorist incident in the process. Police in Evanston, Illinois, a suburb of Chicago, were alerted by residents when they noticed a group in jogging suits making repeated trips to and from a parked van. Two of the group were arrested when they returned to the staked-out vehicle. Nine others were found inside the van along with a large number of weapons.

Among those arrested was Torres, whose father immediately asked that his son be taken in front of an international court, as he considered himself a prisoner of war.

Torres's wife was actually convicted first. She was sentenced to life in prison for planting a bomb that killed a man at a Manhattan office building in 1977.

In 1980, Torres was found guilty of possession of a sawed-off shotgun and conspiracy to commit armed robbery. He received an eight-year sentence. The next year, he was found guilty of seditious conspiracy, armed robbery, weapon violations, and interstate transportation of a stolen vehicle, and was sentenced to seventy years in prison.

Torres, along with nine fellow FALN defendants, refused to participate in the trial, maintaining they were prisoners of war because they were fighting for Puerto Rican independence.

No. 353
LARRY SMITH

First Most Wanted Listing:
July 15, 1977
Apprehended:
August 20, 1977

The FBI said that Larry Smith was a "trigger man" who had been charged in a $1,500 contract killing and, during questioning, reportedly implicated himself in seven other homicides committed during armed robberies.

The Bureau joined the search for Smith after he escaped from a Detroit hospital on May 16, 1977. Smith was in Michigan awaiting trial for the contract killing after being returned from Huntsville, Texas, where he was serving a life sentence for aggravated robbery.

The FBI bulletin said: "Smith, who for years has reportedly been linked to the hierarchy of one of Detroit's most violent street gangs, has been involved in many crimes of a serious nature during his adolescent and adult life. Bearing several bullet-wound scars as a result of his life-style, he has been described by individuals as a 'trigger man' responsible for several homicides. He has many associates in the Detroit metropolitan area and in the past has maintained contact with several of them. Smith normally wears a hat and walks very erect with his head back. He has been employed in the past as a janitor, carpenter and a laborer."

Smith was apprehended on August 20, 1977, by the Toronto Metropolitan Police in Canada. He offered no resistance.

No. 360
THEODORE ROBERT BUNDY

First Most Wanted Listing:
February 10, 1978
Apprehended:
February 15, 1978

Ted Bundy's Most Wanted poster showed a slightly bearded man who was hardly menacing. But the photograph and text gave little hint of the individual who was among the most notorious of all the Most Wanted fugitives.

A suspect in anywhere from 36 to 100 murders, Bundy was finally executed in 1989, more than a decade after he made the Most Wanted List.

The FBI bulletin of February 10, 1978, read: "Theodore Robert Bundy, being sought for a 1975 murder at a ski resort near Aspen, Colorado, has been added to the FBI's list of 'Ten Most Wanted Fugitives.'

"Bundy, who has been convicted of aggravated kidnaping, was awaiting trial for this murder when he escaped from a Colorado jail on December 31, 1977. In addition, he is wanted for questioning in connection with thirty-six similar-type sexual slayings that took place throughout several Western States."

Reports said that Bundy accomplished his jail escape after losing sixty-five pounds in prison, enabling him to slip through a small ventilation opening.

He was arrested in Tallahassee, Florida, where he became a suspect in the murder of two Florida State University coeds. The two women were strangled in their beds; one had been raped. Two other sorority women were also badly beaten. Bundy was eventually tried and convicted of the murders and sentenced to death.

Bundy's execution in the electric chair was actually his sentence for the rape and murder of a twelve-year-old Lake City, Florida, girl in 1978. Credit card receipts were found near the child's body, and several law enforcement authorities theorized that the need to be caught was overwhelming other parts of Bundy's personality.

When all appeals on his behalf had been exhausted and Bundy was finally about to face his execution, he began a series of media interviews and confessions that brought authorities from several states to determine if he had been involved in unsolved murders.

He confessed to twenty more murders, including murders in the states of Washington, Oregon, Idaho, Utah, and Colorado, as well as Florida.

Among his final interviews was a videotaped session in which he described how boyhood glimpses of violent pornography became an "addiction" that grew until his "destructive energy" exploded from fantasy into reality.

Bundy, forty-two at the time of his death, warned that there were others like himself. "There are loose in the towns and their communities people like me today, whose dangerous impulses are being fueled day in, day out, by violence in the media . . . particularly sexual violence.

"I don't want to die, I'm not going to kid you . . . but I deserve certainly the most extreme punishment society has. I think society deserves to be protected from me and from others like me."

No. 362
ANTHONY DOMINIC LIBERATORE

First Most Wanted Listing:
May 26, 1978
Apprehended:
April 1, 1979

One of the few organized crime figures to make the Most Wanted List, Anthony Liberatore held off the Bureau for ten months before his arrest.

Liberatore, a former Cleveland city and labor union official who had spent twenty years in prison for his role in a gang slaying of two Cleveland policemen, reportedly hired contract killers to murder seven underworld opponents. One person was killed by a bomb before the scheme was discovered.

He was arrested when officers broke into his Cleveland home—ten miles from the site of the fatal bombing.

No. 364
CHARLES EVERETT HUGHES

First Most Wanted Listing:
November 19, 1978
Apprehended:
April 29, 1981

When four individuals accidentally interrupted a large-scale smuggling operation in Florida, they paid with their lives. That was the story the FBI told in August 1977 after the bodies of four people, including two teenage sisters, were found weighted with concrete blocks in a sinkhole.

Charles Hughes was named in a federal indictment for unlawful interstate flight to avoid prosecution for murder and intent to distribute a controlled substance. He was identified as the execution-style killer of one adult and the fourteen- and sixteen-year-old sisters and was also wanted on one count of third-degree murder in connection with the shooting death of another adult.

According to the Bureau, the murders occurred on or about January 23, 1977, when the unknowing victims apparently interrupted a drug-smuggling operation in which thirty-five tons of marijuana, with a street value of $1.2 million, was being unloaded. The smuggling operation took place in a remote seacoast area of Bay County, Florida. The bodies of the victims were discovered 100 miles away in August 1977.

According to the FBI, Hughes was known to be a motorcycle enthusiast and mechanic who traveled with his wife, Marilyn. He was arrested without incident on the evening of April 29, 1981, in Myrtle, Mississippi.

No. 365
RONALD LEE LYONS

First Most Wanted Listing:
December 17, 1978
Apprehended:
September 10, 1979

Ronald Lyons was serving a prison sentence in Tennessee for robbery with a deadly weapon when he shot his way to freedom and used an airplane to elude authorities.

In September 1977, Lyons had served five years of a fifty-year sentence at the Turney Correctional Facility in Only, Tennessee. While on an official, after-hours recreational outing with other prisoners and guards at a nearby bowling alley, he and another inmate allegedly produced two sawed-off shotguns, previously hidden in a rest room by coconspirators, and disarmed the guards after a shoot-out. One guard and one other person were injured by gunfire before Lyons, his accomplice, and two other inmates escaped.

The four then embarked on what the FBI called a highly publicized, forty-eight-hour crime spree across western Tennessee during which they took eight hostages and commandeered six vehicles.

The escapees fled the state by forcing the owner of a small airport at Dickson, Tennessee, to take them up in a light aircraft. The flight ended near Moro, Arkansas, when the plane ran low on fuel.

Lyons was arrested by FBI agents who stopped his car near Reno, Nevada. They said he offered no resistance.

No. 367
JOHN WILLIAM SHERMAN

First Most Wanted Listing:
August 3, 1979
Apprehended:
December 17, 1981

The majority of Most Wanted fugitives head underground, severing ties with family and friends and avoiding public contact. John Sherman became a union organizer and even used a federal agency to help him win a $7,200 labor settlement.

Sherman was named to the List after escaping from a prison in Lompoc, California, on April 24, 1979, while serving a thirty-year sentence for bank robbery and escape. While imprisoned, Sherman was taken to downtown Lompoc for treatment by an ophthalmologist. During this visit Sherman retrieved from the rest room a gun that allegedly had been left there by his wife a few hours earlier. He escaped—with his wife driving the getaway car.

The FBI's bulletin said Sherman was a member of the George Jackson Brigade, a revolutionary terrorist organization that claimed credit for a number of bombings and bank robberies on the West Coast of the United States in the 1970s. Sherman was allegedly responsible for fourteen of the bank robberies and eleven bombings.

Sherman was arrested at a gasoline station outside of Denver in 1981. According to reports, he had assumed the name of James Morgan and become a union organizer of Denver-area machinists. A local union official said Sherman was a "brilliant man. It comes as a complete shock to learn who he really was. We knew him as a man with an apparently very high IQ, who seemed to be well-read on virtually any subject you could name."

The official said that Sherman had appeared eighteen months before his arrest and worked in the aviation division at Denver's Sundstrand Corporation. Sherman wanted to organize machinists there.

"We'd been trying to organize the plant for a long time, and we'd always failed," the union official said. "The Teamsters tried, too, without any success. We put Jim on our organization committee." When he was fired from the job, the union charged that he was ousted for union organizing and not because of an inability to do the work. The National Labor Relations Board entered the case, and on his behalf the union brought charges of unfair labor practices against Sundstrand. The company eventually settled out of court by paying "Morgan" $7,200 in back wages.

A week before his arrest, Sherman went to work as a machinist for a small nonunion Denver firm.

Agents said that they were able to track Sherman down not through his own union activity but through his family. Arrested with Sherman were his estranged wife, Marianne, and Paula Jane Botwinick. Mrs. Sherman was charged with aiding her husband's escape. Botwinick was charged with aiding and abetting a fugitive. A meeting at a Seattle hotel between Botwinick and Sherman's mother-in-law led to his arrest, agents said. After the meeting, agents followed Botwinick to Colorado and were eventually led to Sherman.

No. 368
MELVIN BAY GUYON

First Most Wanted Listing:
August 9, 1979
Apprehended:
August 16, 1979

August 9, 1979, stands in infamy in the history of the FBI. On that day three of the Bureau's agents were killed in two separate incidents.

In El Centro, California, a young man who was once investigated as a possible member of the radical Weathermen in the early 1970s walked into the FBI offices and shot and killed two agents before killing himself.

In Cleveland another agent, thirty-five-year-old Johnnie L. Oliver, was killed when he walked into the bedroom of a suspect named Melvin Guyon. After shooting Oliver with a .32 caliber gun, Guyon escaped from five other agents by diving through a small window and fleeing on foot, bleeding profusely from a cut inflicted by broken glass. Minutes later, Guyon stole a bicycle from his landlady thirty blocks away.

Guyon was wanted by Chicago authorities for aggravated kidnaping, armed robbery, and rape.

Guyon was arrested by FBI agents at Southside General Hospital in Youngstown, Ohio, a week later, shortly after a gun battle with agents on a street corner in Youngstown's Southside.

No. 370
EARL EDWIN AUSTIN

First Most Wanted Listing:
October 12, 1979
Apprehended:
March 1, 1980

Earl Austin had a system to rob banks and stuck with it until he had a haul of over a quarter of a million dollars.

According to the FBI, Austin would enter a bank and, impersonating a Federal Deposit Insurance Corporation investigator, request to see the president or manager under the pretext of checking the alarm system. He would then produce a demand note from his briefcase, at the same time displaying a firearm in the waistband of his trousers.

After he gained access to the vault, Austin would empty it and leave the bank with the president or manager as his prisoner. Once outside, he would release the prisoner and escape in a getaway vehicle.

The FBI said that Austin was positively identified in six bank robberies throughout Florida, Alabama, and Kentucky, in which he collected $270,000 in loot. The Bureau's bulletin to law enforcement agencies said that Austin had an extensive criminal record dating back to 1958 and had been convicted of grand larceny, forgery, aggravated assault and battery, bank robbery, escape, and threatening the life of a former president of the United States.

Austin was arrested by FBI agents and local police officers in Tucson, Arizona. He was armed with a 9mm semiautomatic pistol, but the arrest was conducted without incident.

The 1970s
Rogues' Gallery

No. 305
JAMES JOHN BYRNES

First Most Wanted Listing:
January 6, 1970
Apprehended:
April 17, 1970

An accomplished pilot, Byrnes escaped from a jail in St. John, Kansas, by overpowering a jailer. He then stole a car and kidnaped a motorist in Arkansas. He stole an airplane and kidnaped a pilot in Missouri and abandoned the plane and kidnap victims in Iowa. On his FBI release, Byrnes was noted to be a saxophone player who had played in bands in and out of prison.

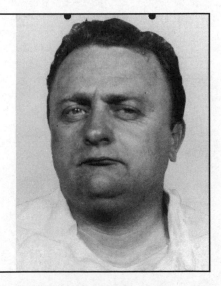

No. 306
EDMUND JAMES DEVLIN

First Most Wanted Listing:
March 20, 1970
Apprehended:
August 15, 1970

"Well known in underworld circles," according to the FBI, Devlin was sought for the $106,333 robbery of a Connecticut trust. He had reputedly been active in numerous criminal activities, including gambling and loan-sharking.

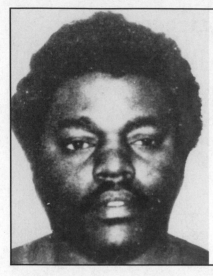

No. 326
JOHN EDWARD COPELAND, JR.

First Most Wanted Listing:
August 15, 1974
Apprehended:
July 23, 1975

According to the FBI bulletin, Copeland was a "paunchy accused sex deviate who, along with an accomplice, allegedly participated in multiple rapes, robberies and kidnapings in California during mid-1973." Brandishing a 12-gauge shotgun and a small automatic pistol, Copeland and his companion allegedly picked up female hitchhikers and took them to isolated beach areas where the victims were terrorized and subjected to repeated rapes and other "aberrations" over extended periods of time.

On one occasion a female hitchhiker and her male friend were reportedly picked up by Copeland and his associate. After allegedly raping the woman repeatedly, Copeland is said to have taken the shotgun he was holding and forced the male victim to place the barrel in his mouth. Copeland pulled the trigger, but the shotgun failed to fire. The two victims were then left alone on the beach after a seven-hour ordeal.

MOST WANTED

No. 329
BILLY DEAN ANDERSON

First Most Wanted Listing:
January 21, 1975
Apprehended:
July 7, 1979

A fugitive "mountain man," Anderson was killed in a shootout with FBI agents outside his mother's home after hiding out in caves in Tennessee's hill country for five years. Anderson had been sought after fleeing to avoid charges of attempted first-degree murder, attempted burglary, and bank robbery. He was alleged to have shot and seriously wounded a deputy sheriff responding to a burglary call.

No. 331
RICHARD DEAN HOLTAN

First Most Wanted Listing:
April 18, 1975
Apprehended:
July 12, 1975

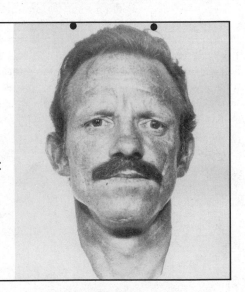

Arrested and placed in a resident release program after a bank robbery, Holtan escaped in 1974 and, only months later, was allegedly involved in the armed robbery of a bar in Omaha, Nebraska. Holtan allegedly forced the bartender and two patrons into a rest room and had the bartender tie up the two customers, after which he fired repeatedly and without provocation at all three. Two of the bullets struck the bartender in the head, killing him, and a third bullet wounded the female patron in the upper shoulder. He then took over $800 from the cash register and calmly left the premises.

No. 333
WILLIAM LEWIS HERRON, JR.

First Most Wanted Listing:
August 15, 1975
Apprehended:
October 30, 1975

Described by the FBI as a "vicious, cunning, professional killer," Herron was wanted in connection with the kidnaping of a prison guard and fellow inmate during his escape from the Kentucky State Prison. While serving a life term for first-degree murder, Herron and another inmate were transported to a medical clinic. On the return trip Herron reportedly produced a .38 caliber revolver, disarmed the guard, and forced him to drive the state-owned vehicle to an isolated area. There he forced the guard and his fellow inmate, who refused to go along with the escape plan, out of the vehicle and shackled them to a tree.

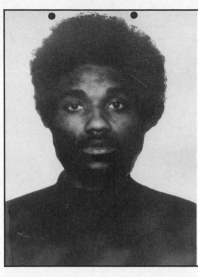

No. 334
JAMES WINSTON SMALLWOOD

First Most Wanted Listing:
August 29, 1975
Apprehended:
December 5, 1975

Smallwood was wanted after his escape from custody while serving a sentence totaling thirty years for two bank robberies. As he was being transported to a courtroom, Smallwood reportedly produced a .32 caliber revolver and held it to the head of the US marshal who was escorting him. He then forced the marshal to park the vehicle they were traveling in, disarmed him, and fired a shot at him before escaping.

No. 336
PATRICK JAMES HUSTON

First Most Wanted Listing:
March 3, 1976
Apprehended:
December 7, 1977

Huston, who had a tattoo reading "In Memory of Mom" on his upper right arm, was wanted in connection with the robbery of the First National City

Bank in Queens, New York, on September 6, 1974. Huston and two accomplices were arrested the same day and charged with the crime, but all three escaped on March 16, 1975.

No. 337
THOMAS EDWARD BETHEA

First Most Wanted Listing:
March 5, 1976
Apprehended:
May 4, 1976

While on parole for a 1971 bank robbery conviction, Bethea was allegedly involved in a kidnaping. A ransom was paid for the safe return of the victim.

No. 340
JAMES RAY RENTON

First Most Wanted Listing:
April 7, 1976
Apprehended:
May 9, 1977

Renton was sought for parole violation, bond default, and unlawful interstate flight to avoid prosecution for the murder of a policeman.

MOST WANTED

No. 341
NATHANIEL DOYLE, JR.

First Most Wanted Listing:
April 29, 1976
Apprehended:
July 15, 1976

A fine dresser who passed himself off as a former professional football player, Doyle was shot and killed by Seattle police officers during a shoot-out following the robbery of a Bellevue, Washington, bank. He was sought on charges of bank robbery and armed robbery after allegedly engaging in a gun battle with California police authorities following a bank robbery in that state.

No. 342
MORRIS LYNN JOHNSON

First Most Wanted Listing:
May 25, 1976
Apprehended:
June 26, 1976

Johnson was sought for bank robbery, bank burglary, parole violation, and escape from a federal prison.

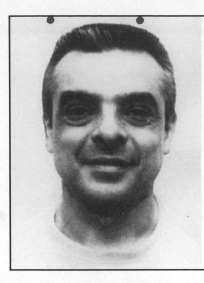

No. 345
GERHARDT JULIUS SCHWARTZ

First Most Wanted Listing:
November 18, 1976
Apprehended:
November 22, 1976

Schwartz and two accomplices were allegedly involved in the robbery of a Rochester, New York, savings and loan. Schwartz's two accomplices were arrested before he made the Most Wanted List. One of them had been brutally stabbed by Schwartz and left for dead shortly following the armed robbery of a local supermarket. A tattoo on Schwartz's left upper arm read "True love, Mom and Dad, 1946."

No. 346
FRANCIS JOHN MARTIN

First Most Wanted Listing:
December 17, 1976
Apprehended:
February 17, 1977

Martin and three accomplices were said to have escaped from the Delaware Correctional Center in Smyrna, Delaware, and to have participated in a kidnaping-rape crime spree in which a young woman was brutally slain. Martin was arrested without incident in Newport Beach, California.

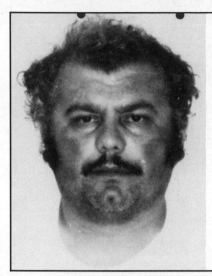

No. 347
BENJAMIN GEORGE PAVAN

First Most Wanted Listing:
January 12, 1977
Apprehended:
February 17, 1977

In San Francisco and Burlingame, California, Pavan had been indicted on charges including five armed robberies, three safe burglaries, grand auto theft, and receiving stolen property. The FBI release on Pavan listed his nine aliases: Joseph Benjamin Costa, J. Costini, Louis Landerini, Ben Panalli, Benjamin Louis Pavan, Benny Pavan, Lou Pavan, Louis Benjamin Pavan, and Joseph Spinelli.

No. 348
LARRY GENE CAMPBELL

First Most Wanted Listing:
March 18, 1977
Apprehended:
September 6, 1977

Campbell was sought after he allegedly murdered two college students in upstate New York.

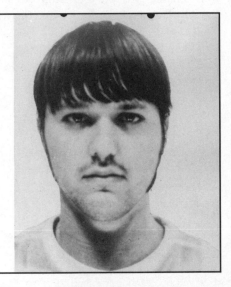

No. 349
ROY ELLSWORTH SMITH

First Most Wanted Listing:
March 18, 1977
Apprehended:
June 2, 1977

Smith, who had been convicted of statutory rape, was wanted for interstate flight to avoid prosecution for the murder of two children.

No. 352
WILLIE FOSTER SELLERS

First Most Wanted Listing:
June 14, 1977
Apprehended:
June 20, 1979

Sellers was sought by the FBI after he escaped from a federal prison in Atlanta. He had been convicted of bank robbery, forgery, and a federal firearms violation.

No. 354
RALPH ROBERT COZZOLINO

First Most Wanted Listing:
October 19, 1977
Apprehended:
January 6, 1978

During an armed robbery of a Chattanooga, Tennessee, food store in August 1977, Cozzolino allegedly shot and killed a police officer in cold blood when the officer entered the store during the robbery.

No. 355
MILLARD OSCAR HUBBARD

First Most Wanted Listing:
October 19, 1977
Apprehended:
October 21, 1977

The alleged participant in four bank robberies, Hubbard and an accomplice took $105,000 from a Tennessee bank after tying the employees to the furniture. As they fled the scene of the crime, the pair fired shots at pursuing police officers.

No. 357
ENRIQUE ESTRADA

First Most Wanted Listing:
December 5, 1977
Apprehended:
December 8, 1977

Estrada was said by the FBI to be a known drug user with an extensive record. He allegedly entered one Hollywood, California, residence in October 1976 and another a month later. Each time, the elderly women victims were robbed, bound, brutally beaten, and left to die.

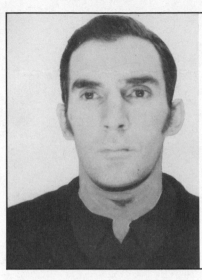

No. 358
WILLIAM DAVID SMITH

First Most Wanted Listing:
February 10, 1978
Apprehended:
October 27, 1978

Smith was listed as a thirty-five-year-old habitual criminal who was believed to have shot his former wife's husband and burned the body in Flint, Michigan, in April 1977. He was also sought for bank robbery and parole violation.

No. 359
GARY RONALD WARREN

First Most Wanted Listing:
February 10, 1978
Apprehended:
May 12, 1978

Warren was sought in connection with a series of armed bank robberies in Florida, West Virginia, Missouri, and California. Before escaping from a Florida prison, he was serving a forty-year sentence for armed robbery.

No. 361
ANDREW EVAN GIPSON

First Most Wanted Listing:
March 27, 1978
Apprehended:
May 24, 1979

Gipson was serving six terms of forty to ninety years under a habitual criminal law when he escaped from the state penitentiary in Lansing, Kansas, in July 1977. He had been imprisoned since 1968, after being convicted of a bank robbery during which a state trooper was shot and killed.

No. 369
GEORGE ALVIN BRUTON

First Most Wanted Listing:
September 28, 1979
Apprehended:
December 14, 1979

About one month after his release from the US Penitentiary at Leavenworth, Kansas, where he had served a six-year sentence for possession of an unregistered firearm and concealing and storing explosives, Bruton and a fellow inmate began a crime spree with the burglary of a drug store. Days later, Bruton fled, after allegedly stealing automobiles, holding hostages, and wounding two law enforcement officers. He was next alleged to have moved in with another former inmate in Kansas City, Missouri. Two months later, the former inmate's body was found. His girlfriend's body was also discovered. Bruton became a suspect in both cases.

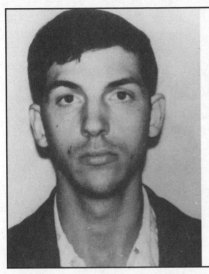

No. 371
VINCENT JAMES RUSSO

First Most Wanted Listing:
December 24, 1979
Apprehended:
January 4, 1981

Russo was sought by the FBI in connection with the armed robbery of a liquor store on December 22, 1978, in Ramona, California. During the robbery a clerk was abducted, forced to the ground, wished a "Merry Christmas," and shot repeatedly at point-blank range with a .45 caliber pistol. Russo was later arrested without incident at his residence in Beaver Falls, Pennsylvania.

The 1980s

Introduction

The 1980s saw a dramatic change in the Most Wanted program, a change that had begun even before the new decade. In 1979 the US Marshal's Office began to assume more responsibility for apprehending fugitives, and the FBI was able to shift its resources to other areas.

"Twenty years ago in some offices, everything would have come to a stop if a substantial lead had come in on a Ten Tenner," said a Bureau spokesman earlier in the decade. "Now we just don't have the manpower because of the expansion of our investigative responsibilities into such areas as narcotics."

The FBI's new areas of investigation spilled over into the Most Wanted List as well. Suspected drug dealers, such as former Miami policeman Armando Garcia, were being added to the Most Wanted List, and the government's RICO statute—racketeer influence and corrupt organizations—was used to charge suspects.

Organizations such as FALN, the Puerto Rican independence movement, and the Order, a neo-Nazi group, also found their members added to the Most Wanted List.

Early in the decade, law enforcement officials had agreed that the Most Wanted program appeared to be suffering both from a lessening of interest by the news media and the proliferation of other Most Wanted programs by organizations such as the US Marshal's Office, the Royal Canadian Mounted Police, and even local police departments.

But when a new television program entitled "America's Most Wanted" appeared on the Fox TV network, it ignited renewed nationwide interest in the Most Wanted List. No sooner had the program begun its regular schedule, than a TV viewer recognized a Most Wanted fugitive who had been featured, and the first of several arrests were made from tips sparked by the show.

No. 372
ALBERT VICTORY

First Most Wanted Listing:
March 14, 1980
Apprehended:
February 24, 1981

The first addition to the Most Wanted List in the 1980s was a prison escapee serving a twenty-five-year to life sentence for the murder of a New York City patrolman.

Albert Victory escaped from the Greenhaven, New York, Correctional Facility on May 5, 1978, with the assistance of three armed companions.

When Victory was added to the Most Wanted List in 1980, the FBI said that he reportedly had been employed since his escape as a "strongarm" and loan shark collector for organized crime.

Less than a year later, Victory was arrested without incident by local and federal authorities at his residence in Lafayette, California.

**No. 374
DANIEL JAY BARNEY**

First Most Wanted Listing:
March 10, 1981
Committed Suicide:
April 19, 1981

Brothers Daniel and Joseph Barney were wanted for a series of crimes in which they were both accused of sexual assault and burglary.

The FBI said that the pair often worked together. They attempted to gain entry into a young woman's residence and then assaulted the victim repeatedly. The attacks usually lasted longer than three hours. One of the assailants always acted dominant, the other was apologetic. The brothers then often took valuable items they saw.

The pair was wanted for a trail of crimes in California, Wyoming, and Nevada. Daniel Barney was added to the Most Wanted List just over a year after escaping from a jail in Jefferson County, Wisconsin, where he had been held on a sexual assault charge. A karate expert, he was considered the more violent of the two men.

Daniel Barney shot himself in the heart after he had broken into a Denver condominium and held a woman hostage. Authorities said that Barney entered the condominium at 5 A.M. through an unlocked back door and went into a bedroom where a couple was sleeping. He tied up the man and took the woman to another bedroom.

About an hour later, the man cut himself free with a knife in his pocket and ran to a neighbor's home to call the police, who went inside and tried to convince Barney to free the woman.

Police and Barney talked for more than two hours, and all the while he kept a .38 caliber revolver cocked and pointed at his chest. When he asked a detective to give his mother a message, the detective replied he didn't know his name. Barney told him he would find out soon enough.

He told them his brother had been shot in the heart at 8:20 A.M. and that was the time "he wanted to go."

Police assumed he wanted to give up when he said he wanted to put on a shirt and go to the bathroom. He returned to the top of the stairs, knelt, looked at his watch, and shot himself. Authorities said they were puzzled about the reference to his brother.

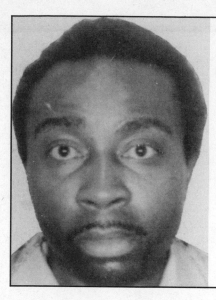

No. 377
LESLIE NICHOLS

First Most Wanted Listing:
July 2, 1981
Apprehended:
December 17, 1981

Heavily involved in narcotics trafficking since his teenage years, Leslie Nichols joined the Most Wanted List in connection with the drug-related, execution-style murders of four people in Little Rock, Arkansas, during June 1980.

Thirty-eight at the time, Nichols was sought by the FBI after a warrant was issued charging him with interstate flight to avoid prosecution for the crime of capital murder.

The victims were thought to have been murdered over a four-day period. In each instance their hands and feet were tied with coat-hanger wire, and they were shot at close range in the back of the head. One victim was found in the backseat of a car; two others were discovered in the trunk of another car; the fourth was found in a ditch.

In addition, the FBI said that Nichols was wanted for questioning about two other murders in Chicago.

He was arrested by FBI agents and local police at a Los Angeles apartment on December 17, 1981. The Bureau said the arrest occurred without incident.

No. 378
THOMAS WILLIAM MANNING

First Most Wanted Listing:
January 29, 1982
Apprehended:
April 24, 1985

The Mannings seemed like an average American family. Thomas Manning, born in 1946, was handy around the house, and lived happily with his wife and their three small children.

But on January 29, 1982, the illusion was shattered when Manning was added to the Most Wanted List. He was sought in connection with the murder of a New Jersey state trooper in 1981 and a series of bank robberies in Maine.

At the time of his listing, Manning was said to be traveling with his wife, Carol Ann Manning, twenty-six at the time, an eight-year-old son, a two-year-old daughter, and an infant son. Also said to be with the family was Richard Charles Williams, who had also been charged in the murder of the New Jersey state trooper. A close associate of Manning's was said to be Raymond Luc Levasseur, who had made the Most Wanted List in 1977 as number 350.

The group made up a portion of what became known as the Sam Melville–Jonathan Jackson Unit and the United Freedom Front, which, according to a US attorney, participated in a nine-year conspiracy of bombing, murder, and bank robbery and conspired to overthrow the US government.

The first substantial break in the case came when heavily armed teams of FBI agents and local police officers raided homes in Cleveland and Deerfield, a small farming town south of Cleveland.

Both Levasseur and Williams were arrested. During the arrests the authorities came up with a telephone number they suspected belonged to the

Mannings. Sixteen hours later, agents descended on a home in New Lyme, Ohio.

The house was deserted. The "Carr" family had departed so hastily that they had left behind their Great Dane and, in a trunk in a bedroom, the 9mm pistol that had been used to shoot the state trooper eight times.

The Mannings had apparently fooled everyone who knew them in Ohio. Their children were later said to have been model students. At the time of the mid-November raid, their home was decorated with three jack-o'-lanterns, dry corn stalks, and a scarecrow.

The Mannings managed to avoid arrest for another six months, living quietly in a middle-class neighborhood in Norfolk, Virginia.

Carol Manning was apprehended first, at a shopping center a mile from their new home. Ten minutes later, the FBI descended on Thomas Manning. "He was lying down in the yard sunning," said an arresting agent. "We caught him totally unaware." Manning offered no resistance.

A month later, a federal grand jury indicted Thomas Manning, thirty-nine, and Carol Manning, thirty-one, on conspiracy charges for the murder of the state trooper, attempted murder of three other police officers, nineteen bombings and attempted bombings, and ten bank robberies to fund their conspiracy.

In January 1987 Manning was found guilty of felony murder, which is committing homicide while committing another felony. The following month, he was sentenced to life in prison, without a chance of parole for the next thirty years.

No. 379
MUTULU SHAKUR

First Most Wanted Listing:
July 23, 1982
Apprehended:
February 11, 1986

It took nearly five years, but the FBI finally brought in the fugitive who, they said at the time of his Most Wanted listing, was a "major subject" in an aborted armored car robbery in Nanuet, New York, in 1981 during which one guard and two police officers were killed.

Mutulu Shakur, born Jeral Wayne Williams in Baltimore, Maryland, was added to the Most Wanted List after most of the other principals from the incident had been arrested—and in some cases, convicted of crimes.

Authorities said three gunmen wearing ski masks had opened fire at the rear of a Brink's truck that was stopped at the Nanuet National Bank to pick up three bags of cash. One guard was killed and two others wounded.

The gunmen fled after taking six bags of money carrying a reported $1.6 million; they hooked up with several accomplices nearby, fleeing in a van and a small car. The van was stopped by a roadblock, where officers pulled the driver and a passenger from the vehicle.

Three people with guns fired shots at the police, and two officers—one, thirty-two years old; the other, forty-five—died a short time later. A third officer suffered a flesh wound.

Four of the robbers stole two cars from bystanders and escaped, but an off-duty New York City corrections officer arrested a fifth as she ran from the scene. The woman turned out to be Katherine Boudin, a Weather Underground fugitive who had been sought for more than ten years, since a bomb explosion leveled a Greenwich Village, New York, town house. Three people were killed in the blast.

Three other suspects, all New York City residents who had fled Nanuet in the car, were caught in Nyack after their vehicle crashed. Arrested were Judith Clark, James Lester Hackford, and Solomon Quienes.

A search of their homes provided authorities with a treasure chest of information about the Weather Underground, which one newspaper report called "a group of 1960s anti-war radicals and 1970s anti-establishment bomb-builders who managed to elude capture for 10 years."

At their homes were lists of names, police station floor plans, guns, and bomb-making equipment. For the police, resources that had rarely worked in the hunt for these fugitives—fingerprints, license plate numbers, search warrants—began to pay off. Soon, several more members of the group were arrested.

Shakur's role was made public in 1982, at the same time he was added to the List. Federal indictments said he was the founder of a Harlem clinic that the Brink's robbery group used as its headquarters. It went on to say that Shakur had been identified by FBI informants as "directing the planning discussions" for the Brink's heist, which the group referred to by the code name of "the Big Dane."

The FBI said that seventeen people were involved in the conspiracy to commit the crime, including former members of the Weather Underground and soldiers of the Black Liberation Army.

In October 1983, the first members of the group were sentenced to seventy-five years in prison for what a judge called the cold, calculated, and deliberate murders of three people during the robbery.

In February 1986 Shakur was finally arrested in Los Angeles. He was found guilty of armed robbery, racketeering, and murder charges by a federal jury in 1988.

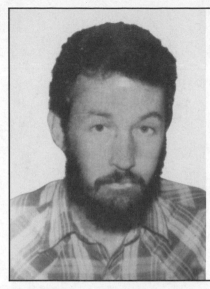

No. 382
LANEY GIBSON, JR.

First Most Wanted Listing:
November 16, 1983
Apprehended:
December 18, 1983

A convicted murderer, Laney Gibson had a habit of escaping jails and committing more murders.

Gibson, in prison on two murder convictions, escaped from the Clay County Jail in Kentucky on August 7, 1983. He was awaiting trial for the brutal shooting of a Manchester, Kentucky, man on February 26, 1981. The man, who was shot in the head with a 9mm handgun, remained paralyzed until his death nearly a year later.

After his escape Gibson was also indicted by authorities in Elgin, Ohio, for the kidnaping and slaying of a postmistress. Officials found an open safe, an empty cash drawer, and the contents of the woman's purse spread on a counter. When she was later found, she had been tortured, raped, and murdered.

A month after making the Most Wanted List, Gibson was arrested by FBI agents and local police in Montgomery, Alabama.

Gibson, however, escaped from prison again in September 1984 but was arrested a few months later hiding in the false ceiling in the house of a relative.

No. 384
SAMUEL MARK HUMPHREY

First Most Wanted Listing:
February 29, 1984
Apprehended:
March 22, 1984

The last place you'd expect a Most Wanted fugitive to visit voluntarily would be a center of justice. That is exactly where Samuel Humphrey was eventually arrested.

Humphrey was named to the Most Wanted List in connection with the 1977 murder of a man in Detroit who allegedly was shot during the robbery of his home. Humphrey was also wanted for two 1983 bank robberies, in Rochester, New York, and Atlanta, Georgia. Additionally, he was wanted for the 1982 armed robbery of a jewelry store in San Diego, California.

Humphrey was described as a heavy user of cocaine and heroin who was known to carry multiple handguns. He was arrested unarmed in the Portland Justice Center, where he had gone to visit an inmate.

Apprehended one block away was his associate Luvenia Marie Carter, who had been wanted for bank robbery and interstate transportation of stolen property.

No. 385
CHRISTOPHER BERNARD WILDER

First Most Wanted Listing:
April 5, 1984
Apprehended:
August 13, 1984

Christopher Wilder pretended to be many things he was not. News reports upon his death seemed to believe the claims, even referring to Wilder as a "wealthy Australian-born playboy" and "race-car driver."

Wilder's stories often were nothing short of believable, enough so that he was able to talk his way out of a charge of molesting a sixteen-year-old in 1977 and of raping a model in 1980.

Wilder received a five-year probation period for the 1980 incident, in which he conned two teenage girls into modeling for him and then raped the one he fancied most. Wilder pleaded guilty to a lesser charge of attempted sexual battery. Ordered to undergo treatment as a condition of probation, he was said to have dutifully attended sessions with a sex therapist until February 1984.

Then Wilder went on a five-week cross-country spree of kidnap, rape, and murder that ended 8,000 miles later after the abduction of at least twelve women, eight of whom have either vanished or been found dead. Wilder would approach young women, saying he was a manager of a local modeling school, and would then offer to drive them around to take their pictures.

Wilder was said by contracting-business associates in Boynton, Florida, to have had a "knack" with women. He was flashy in appearance, wearing expensive-looking rings, leather jackets, and driving a Porsche.

The rings, said one business associate, were fake. The same associate found ironic the accounts that Wilder was "a millionaire Australian race-car driver." His single-bedroom home cost only $62,000. His will listed an approximate worth of $445,100 but did not include considerable debts. His racing "career" consisted of no more than ten races, and he had never finished beyond the halfway point in the pack. Wilder was not Australian, although he had been born in Australia to an Australian mother and an American father, who moved the family to the United States shortly after Wilder's birth.

Wilder's infamous crime spree began on February 26 in Miami, Florida, with the disappearance of a twenty-year-old woman from the Miami Grand Prix auto race, in which he had competed.

On March 5, in Coral Gables, Florida, a twenty-three-year-old woman disappeared. She had last been seen with Wilder at a service station.

On March 18, in Melbourne, Florida, an aspiring model disappeared from a shopping center. Her brutalized body was found in a swamp four days later.

On March 20, in Tallahassee, Florida, the abduction, rape, and torture of a Florida State University student—who escaped in Bainbridge, Georgia— gave police their first description of Wilder.

On March 23, in Beaumont, Texas, Wilder murdered a woman, whose body was found in a ditch three days later.

On March 25, in Oklahoma City, Oklahoma, a twenty-one-year-old woman was abducted from a shopping mall. Her body was discovered by fishermen at Milford Lake, Kansas.

On March 29, in Grand Junction, Colorado, a nineteen-year-old girl disappeared from a shopping center.

On April 1, in Las Vegas, Nevada, a seventeen-year-old girl was last seen leaving a shopping mall with a man fitting Wilder's description.

On April 4, in Torrance, California, a sixteen-year-old girl disappeared. She later turned up alive, saying that she had been forced to drive with Wilder across country. He had abused her along the way, then sent her home on a plane, saying he was going to be killed.

On April 10, in Merrillville, Indiana, a sixteen-year-old girl was abducted after she applied for a job at a shopping mall. She was found near Penn Yan, New York, stabbed but still alive. She later told police that another girl had lured her to Wilder's car.

On April 12, in Phelps, New York, a thirty-three-year-old woman was found slain on a rural road.

Wilder's bloody trail finally ended August 13, in Colebrook, New Hampshire, when his car was spotted by two state patrol officers who had been told by the FBI that Wilder might be in the area. He had been added to the Most Wanted List on April 5.

According to police reports, when the two officers approached the car, Wilder went for a weapon in the glove compartment. One officer jumped him, and Wilder turned the gun on himself. He fired once, and the bullet passed through his body and hit an officer. He fired again and killed himself.

Wilder's former probation officer said, "There were never any signs to pick up on. He was clean-cut, cooperative, personable—never once lost his temper. With hindsight, this whole thing might look like it could have been prevented. But we get a lot of guys like Wilder. He was under care and doing well."

No. 387
WAI-CHU NG

First Most Wanted Listing:
June 15, 1984
Apprehended:
October 4, 1984

When a sixty-one-year-old man crawled into an alley outside the Wah-My Club in Seattle's Chinatown district, the public was alerted to the awful horror inside. Police found that thirteen people, mostly elderly Asian men, had been massacred execution-style at the private gambling club.

The Wah-My Club, which police said they had known about for years, was described as a Chinese private club that was often the scene of high-stakes gambling. Robbery was considered the motive for the three individuals who were said to have committed the crime.

The victims were found hog-tied. Autopsies showed the twelve men and one woman died of one or more gunshot wounds to the head, some nearly point-blank. The lone survivor had been shot in the neck.

Within hours of the worst mass-murder in Seattle's history, two of the three suspects were in custody. Arrested were twenty-year-old Benjamin Ng and twenty-two-year-old Kwan Mak, both Hong Kong natives and residents of Seattle. Police immediately appealed to the Chinese community for help in bringing the third suspect, whose identity was unknown, to justice.

Over a month later, authorities said they filed thirteen counts of aggravated first-degree murder against Wai-Chu Ng, twenty-six, of Seattle, who disappeared the day of the crime.

The FBI added Wai-Chu Ng to the Most Wanted List on June 15, 1984. He was arrested on October 4, 1984, by the Royal Canadian Mounted Police in a high-rise Chinatown apartment in Calgary, Alberta. Authorities who tracked Ng for nineteen months said that standard investigative techniques helped them follow him from Hong King to Canada, where he had been living under an assumed name for eight months.

Trials for the first two defendants ended with a death sentence for Kwan Mak and life imprisonment without parole for Benjamin Ng. Wai-Chu Ng, no relation to Benjamin Ng, received a sentence of thirteen life terms. He had been acquitted of thirteen accounts of first-degree murder—his defense contended he had been coerced into participating by the two other men—but was found guilty of thirteen counts of first-degree robbery and one count of assault.

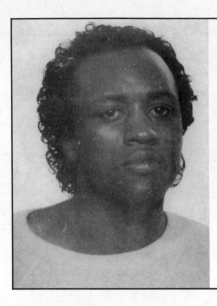

No. 388
ALTON COLEMAN

First Most Wanted Listing:
October 24, 1984
Apprehended:
January 25, 1985

When Alton Coleman was captured, it was big enough news for the *Kenosha Times* in Wisconsin to publish a special Saturday edition devoted entirely to the event.

Coleman had dominated headlines in the Midwest for weeks during a six-state, seven-week criminal rampage that included kidnaping, rape, and murder. Upon his arraignment he was held on bail of $25 million. An assistant US attorney said, "I know of no person in this nation who has ever been a greater flight risk."

Coleman was wanted for:

- The abduction and murder of Vernita Wheat, nine, of Kenosha, who was found strangled June 19, 1984, in an abandoned house in Waukesha, Illinois.
- The abduction of two girls on their way to a grocery store in Gary, Indiana, on June 19. A seven-year-old girl was killed. A nine-year-old was sexually assaulted.
- The kidnaping on June 19 of a twenty-five-year-old Gary woman, whose body was found in an abandoned house in Detroit on July 11.
- The kidnaping on June 24 of a twenty-eight-year-old Detroit woman, who was abducted in her car at knifepoint and ordered to drive to Ohio. She escaped by driving her car into a truck.
- The murder in Toledo, Ohio, of a thirty-year-old-woman and her ten-year-old daughter. Their bodies were found in a crawlspace.
- The murder of a forty-four-year-old woman and the severe beating of her husband in Norwood, Ohio.

- The July 17 beating and robbery of a seventy-nine-year-old minister and his wife. The couple's car was stolen and abandoned two days later. Still missing at the time of Coleman's arrest were the woman and two children, ages three and four, who had been staying with the couple.

Coleman was accompanied in his flight by his girlfriend, Debra Brown. Both were from Waukegan, Illinois, and were arrested in Evanston after police received a tip they were in a local park. The tip, police said, was not anonymous.

The two were confronted while they were sitting on bleachers. Brown got up to walk away when three officers with guns drawn approached. Police said Coleman gave up without a word. He was carrying two knives, one in his back pocket and another in his shoe. Brown, who was caught twenty feet away, had a revolver in her purse.

The arresting officers said they had no problem recognizing Coleman. "You could tell it was him," one said. "We had his picture posted everywhere."

A police profile released after his arrest said that Coleman was a sexually disoriented man who had a strong psychological pull over others but would turn on them without warning. As a boy, Coleman witnessed his mother's sexual relations. His mother later deserted him. He was confused and directionless as a youth, taunted by classmates for wetting his pants. He was described by authorities as a man who, "like any other predator, lurked in the urban areas preying on the weak."

In the first of a series of trials, Coleman was found guilty in June 1985 of the death of a fifteen-year-old Cincinnati youth and was sentenced to death. In all, he received the death sentence in Ohio, Indiana, and Illinois.

The final sentence came in Illinois for the death of Vernita Wheat, the nine-year-old Kenosha girl. Afterward, Coleman said that when he was captured he had been "tired of running, tired of being involved with criminals, tired, period." He said he had a knife in his sock then and could have committed suicide with it.

He added, "I wish I had the strength to commit suicide. You wouldn't see me here today. Punishment is not death in this case. I'm dead already. You're talking to a dead man."

But the case's prosecutor, noting Coleman had said he was tired of running and surrendered to police without struggling, said, "Of course he didn't fight the police. They're men and not too old to defend themselves. He likes to pick on very old people and little children."

Referring to Coleman's statement that he didn't get a fair trial, the prosecutor said, "Alton Coleman didn't give Vernita Wheat a trial."

The same prosecutor called Wheat's mother shortly after the jury voted to recommend Coleman be sentenced to death. "She was ecstatic," he said.

No. 390
CARMINE JOHN PERSICO, JR.

First Most Wanted Listing:
January 31, 1985
Apprehended:
February 15, 1985

Organized crime figures generally did not make the Most Wanted List. Carmine "The Snake" Persico was one of the exceptions—and with good reason.

Persico's Most Wanted poster said he was sought for "Racketeer Influenced and Corrupt Organizations—Bribery, Conspiracy" (the government's famous RICO statute) and for "Bribery of Public Officials."

According to the FBI, Persico was at the time the "fifty-one-year-old reputed boss of one of the largest organized crime families in New York City." The Bureau said that in addition to charges of alleged widespread extortion in the construction and restaurant industries in New York City, Persico had also been sought for reportedly using proceeds from drug trafficking and illegal gambling activities to bribe public officials.

Through these bribes, the Bureau said, he allegedly attempted to prevent criminal tax prosecutions of family members as well as fix court cases and to improve prison conditions for family members. He had already been convicted of lottery law violations, assault, theft from interstate shipment, and conspiracy to bribe an Internal Revenue Service agent.

Persico was arrested in Wantagh, New York, by FBI agents, who said he was unarmed and did not resist.

No. 394
ROBERT HENRY NICOLAUS

First Most Wanted Listing:
June 28, 1985
Apprehended:
July 20, 1985

Robert Nicolaus brutally killed his three children and served time for the crime, but he wasn't through with murder.

The FBI added the fifty-two-year-old ex-convict to the Most Wanted List after his second former wife was shot to death on February 22, 1985. Nicolaus allegedly lured the woman into a Sacramento, California, alley and shot her twice in the chest with a .25 caliber automatic handgun. The woman was reportedly able to name Nicolaus as her assailant before she died nearly a half hour later.

On September 25, 1964, Nicolaus was convicted and sentenced to death for the murders of his two-year-old and seven-year-old daughters and five-year-old son. Nicolaus reportedly gathered the children together on May 24, 1964, and went to a Sacramento toy store, where he bought them numerous toys and gifts.

He then took them to a deserted field and had them climb into the trunk of his car on the pretext of looking for a lost key. As they searched the trunk, Nicolaus pulled out a .38 caliber revolver and shot them repeatedly in the back of the head. Due to a revision in California law, Nicolaus's sentence was reduced in 1967, and he was paroled from prison on August 15, 1977.

The FBI said that Nicolaus had been an author, economic analyst, and gardener in the past. He was reportedly quite familiar with rifles and shotguns and had a fondness for old-model Rambler automobiles. He also was reportedly an avid jogger who lifted weights and frequented health-food stores.

Nicolaus was apprehended unarmed and without incident in York, Pennsylvania, by members of the FBI and local police.

No. 396
RICHARD JOSEPH SCUTARI

First Most Wanted Listing:
September 30, 1985
Apprehended:
March 19, 1986

Richard Scutari was a member of the Order, which the FBI said was "a violent terrorist group which advocates the assassination of government leaders, overthrow of the U.S. Government and white supremacy."

Scutari was sought for his alleged involvement in an armored truck robbery in Ukiah, California, in which $3.6 million was stolen; in connection with the interstate transportation of over $5,000 in stolen money; and for storing and concealing approximately $40,000 in stolen money.

Scutari was also thought to have been involved in the June 1984 murder of talk-show host Alan Berg, assassinated outside his Denver home by a gunman who fired thirteen bullets into him with an automatic weapon. Berg, who was Jewish, had a reputation for insulting white supremacists and their beliefs on his program.

Within months, a federal jury in Seattle had convicted ten members of the neo-Nazi group of racketeering in what the prosecution said was a white supremacist plot that included Berg's murder and more than $4 million in robberies in 1983 and 1984.

According to testimony in the trial, Order members were assigned assassination targets such as prominent Jews and television network presidents, who were considered enemies of the white race. The group was following the plot of *The Turner Diaries,* a white supremacist novel that depicts a band of Aryan warriors waging war against the government and financing their efforts through armored-car robberies and counterfeiting, and in which the federal government is referred to as ZOG—the Zionist Occupied Government.

Despite the convictions, the jury stopped short of declaring who had actually murdered Berg. Scutari, who was listed after the trial as the only remaining living member of the team that killed Berg, was still at large. He was named Most Wanted fugitive number 396 on September 30, 1985. The FBI said that Scutari had been a karate instructor and was "reportedly armed with unlimited ammunition, weapons, and is known to use bullet-proof vests." The Bureau also said, "He has vowed not to be taken alive."

Scutari was tracked to San Antonio, Texas, where FBI special agents arrested him without incident, saying he was unarmed. He was later acquitted of federal charges of violating civil rights in the murder of Berg.

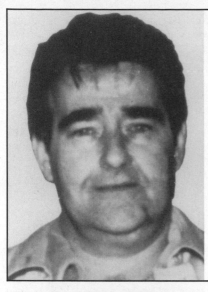

No. 397
JOSEPH WILLIAM DOUGHERTY

First Most Wanted Listing:
November 6, 1985
Apprehended:
December 19, 1986

No. 402
TERRY LEE CONNOR

First Most Wanted Listing:
August 8, 1986
Apprehended:
December 9, 1986

The two men who arrived at the door of a bank executive's home in suburban Milwaukee, Wisconsin, in September 1985 were dressed in suits, carried briefcases, and identified themselves as US marshals. But the pair pulled guns from their briefcases and very politely said, "We're aren't here to display our badges. We are here to rob the bank."

The men held the executive, his wife, his daughter, and his daughter's boyfriend overnight at their home and then, in the morning, drove them to the bank in the family's van. After forcing the executive to let them into the bank, the men robbed the vault and two night-deposit boxes. Bank employees who came to work during the robbery also were held hostage, but no one was injured.

Just two months later, the FBI named Joseph Dougherty, the first of two individuals involved with the crime, to the Most Wanted List. Dougherty was said to have been accompanied by Terry Connor. The FBI said that the pair had escaped from US marshals on June 19, 1985, while being transported to federal court in Oklahoma.

The FBI said that after the escape the pair began a series of bank robberies throughout Missouri and Nevada, as well as in Wisconsin. Connor was added to the Most Wanted List in August 1986. Connor was arrested first, in Chicago. Dougherty was arrested in Antioch, California.

The pair were tried in federal court in Milwaukee and found guilty of several crimes in connection with the hostage-taking incident. Already sentenced to two life terms and 124 years imprisonment for other incidents, they were each given an additional life term without parole and ordered to pay restitution of $527,000, the take in the Milwaukee robbery.

The bank executive said at the trial that since the incident, he and his family never left a door unlocked behind them and that the family still suffered from effects of the crime. They were, however, "elated" at the outcome.

Before the sentencing, Dougherty told the judge that already he had prison terms that would not expire until August 26, 2132, one day after his 193rd birthday. The judge, however, called the robbery "an outrageous crime. In a civilized society, to hold people hostage for ransom is one of the worst things that can happen."

No. 399
BILLY RAY WALDON

First Most Wanted Listing:
May 16, 1986
Apprehended:
June 16, 1986

Billy Waldon was added to the Most Wanted List after a violent crime spree in California that included attempted murder, murder, rape, robbery, burglary, and arson.

He was sought in connection with the murders of a forty-three-year-old woman and her fourteen-year-old daughter in San Diego, whose badly burned bodies were discovered on December 7, 1985, after their home had been set on fire. Autopsies revealed that the daughter died as a result of the fire and her mother from a broken neck caused by a .25 caliber bullet.

Waldon was also wanted in connection with what the FBI called a "brutal" rape of a San Diego woman on December 17, 1985, and the robbery of another San Diego woman on December 20, 1985. He was also a suspect in a series of robberies and burglaries that occurred in October and November 1985 in Tulsa, Oklahoma. During the spree in Tulsa, five victims were injured and a fifty-year-old woman was killed as a result of gunshot wounds.

The FBI bulletin said Waldron reportedly spoke Esperanto, French, Italian, Japanese, and Spanish, was one-quarter Cherokee Indian, and had demonstrated "an interest in his history." The bulletin also said, "He has also shown interest in the subject of Acquired Immune Deficiency Syndrome, better known as AIDS, and may have homosexual tendencies."

He was apprehended by San Diego police officers who tried to stop him for a routine traffic citation concerning a faulty brake light. Waldron reportedly dropped a .357 Magnum revolver while attempting to flee from the pursuing officers on foot. He was positively identified through fingerprints after his arrest.

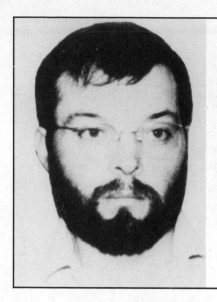

No. 400
CLAUDE LAFAYETTE DALLAS, JR.

First Most Wanted Listing:
May 16, 1986
Apprehended:
March 8, 1987

Some people in the Far West of the United States thought that Claude Dallas, Jr., had done what comes naturally when someone draws a gun on them—he shot first.

The FBI, however, released a strongly worded bulletin that differed with that version: Dallas had brutally killed two Idaho game wardens who had attempted to arrest him. FBI Director William H. Webster was quoted in the Bureau's bulletin: "There are those who look upon Dallas as a folk hero. However, the murders of two Fish and Game officers were committed by a dangerous and vicious man, who has no regard for society's laws. Those who so casually reject our laws are criminals—not heroes. I'm certain the citizens of Idaho and the entire country will join us in our search for this fugitive from justice."

The FBI named Dallas Most Wanted fugitive number 400 after he escaped from the Idaho State Penitentiary on March 30, 1986, while serving a thirty-year sentence for voluntary manslaughter. Dallas had been convicted of killing the two wardens, fifty-year-old Bill Pogue and thirty-four-year-old Conley Elms, by shooting them numerous times before, the FBI said, "summarily executing them with a .22-caliber rifle shot through the temple."

The two officers had gone to Dallas's remote trapping camp in southwestern Idaho to investigate reports that Dallas was hunting deer and trapping bobcats out of season.

According to testimony at his trial, after he shot the men, Dallas threw Elms's body into a river and, with the help of a friend, loaded Pogue's body into a pickup truck. He drove into the northern Nevada desert alone and buried the body, which was not found until Dallas later testified where he had buried it.

Dallas's mastery of survival skills in the wild enabled him to elude authorities for nearly fourteen months while he traveled through the desolate region where Nevada, Oregon, and Idaho meet. He was also helped by friends; they left their pickups—with full gas tanks and keys in the ignitions—in the northern Nevada desert for him and would leave food at night as well.

A writer who followed the case for a local magazine said, "I was struck by the way people looked at Dallas, in contrast to the way they would look at any other killer. People automatically assumed that if this hard-working man killed two game wardens, somehow the game wardens had to be at fault."

Dallas was finally captured by FBI agents in April 1982, after a shoot-out and chase ending in Paradise Valley, Nevada. The apprehension followed a lengthy chase across the desert, with Dallas in a pickup truck and FBI agents in a chartered aircraft, a Huey helicopter, and Bureau vehicles. Dallas, armed with a .30-30 rifle, a .22 caliber pistol, and a .357 revolver, received minor wounds during an exchange of gunfire.

While charged with two counts of first-degree murder, Dallas claimed that he was acting in self-defense in that Pogue had threatened to kill him and that Pogue drew his gun first. His attorney said in final arguments that Dallas was "a man who had sought only protection of his home, his property, the preservation of his life."

The jury found him guilty of two counts of voluntary manslaughter. The jury foreman said the two wardens seemed to be overstepping their duties by insisting on arresting Dallas for poaching. "We just thought the wardens were overbearing." While concluding he had legitimate fear for his life, however, the jury reasoned he lost his claim to self-defense because he shot the two men more than once.

On March 30, 1986, Dallas escaped from prison—to the surprise of few—by cutting through two heavy-gauge chain-link fences. "Everybody said they knew he was going to escape," said the prison warden. "Even his lawyer, when we told him, said, 'I kinda figured on that.' Of everybody I did not want to escape, he's on the top of that list."

Dallas's second flight from authorities did not last long. On March 8, 1987, Dallas was arrested peacefully at a convenience store in Riverside, California, where he apparently had friends. In 1986 his story, already a book, was turned into a TV movie, which many critics said incorrectly romanticized the killer.

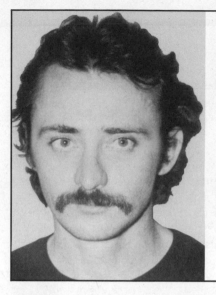

No. 403
FILLMORE RAYMOND CROSS, JR.

First Most Wanted Listing:
August 8, 1986
Apprehended:
December 23, 1986

Fillmore Cross's FBI background sketch said he was reportedly "one of the most influential members of the Hell's Angels Motorcycle Club in the United States."

A founding member of the San Jose, California, chapter of the Hell's Angels, Cross became the object of an FBI manhunt after a federal warrant was issued for unlawful interstate flight. The charge followed an incident in which a California businessman was nearly beaten to death by two individuals whom Cross allegedly hired. The FBI claimed Cross was trying to extort $100,000 from the businessman.

The FBI described Cross as an avid weight lifter who had highly developed upper arms and forearms. They said he reportedly was trained in the martial arts and sometimes carried a handgun in an ankle holster.

His interests, the Bureau said, included motorcycles, ancient Mexican artifacts, wine, expensive automobiles, and rattlesnakes. Among his previous jobs were bail bondsman, car salesman, collector, construction worker, import business owner, real estate investor, and tree surgeon. Among his nicknames and aliases were Fill Raymond Close, Fillmore Cross, Phillip Raymond Cross, Gary Greenfest, Phillip Louis Long, Walter Lee McMillen, Carl Westmore, Fill, and Pierre.

Cross voluntarily surrendered to FBI agents in San Francisco, California.

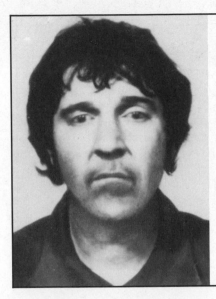

No. 406
MIKE WAYNE JACKSON

First Most Wanted Listing:
October 1, 1986
Apprehended:
October 2, 1986

Mike Jackson had been in trouble with the authorities for most of his life when a routine visit to his home by a parole officer somehow set him off on a multistate rampage of terror and death.

Jackson, paroled from the Medical Center for Federal Prisons in Springfield, Missouri, on April 14, 1986, was visited at his Indianapolis, Indiana, residence by his parole officer. During the visit, Jackson brandished a sawed-off 12-gauge, pump-action shotgun and fatally wounded the officer, with shots to the leg, chest, and head.

A woman witness said that she heard a noise at Jackson's house and saw him pointing a shotgun at the officer. "Don't do it! Don't do it," the officer was heard to say. A moment later, the woman said, Jackson fired the shotgun and the officer fell. Jackson then walked over to the victim, racked the shotgun, shouldered the weapon, leaned over, and shot the officer again.

He then reportedly smeared grease on his face, spray-painted his face and hair with silver paint, and allegedly began his crime spree. When the FBI added Jackson to the Most Wanted List, the charges included two additional killings, five abductions, three attempted abductions, robbery, attempted murder, assault with a deadly weapon, the wounding of a police officer, and seven auto thefts. Jackson had been arrested more than thirty times in seventeen years and had numerous convictions. He had also had a history of heroin use, alcohol abuse, and schizophrenia.

His next crime, according to the FBI, was in an Indianapolis convenience store. When an employee did not move fast enough, Jackson reportedly shot him in the throat and left him to die.

Jackson then reportedly ordered a truck driver to take him to the airport, where he forced the driver out and stole the truck. Jackson then reportedly robbed another individual and stole his truck. He abandoned the vehicle and forced an Indianapolis woman to drive him north to Frankfort, Indiana, where she escaped after jumping from her car.

In Frankfort, Jackson abducted a woman and her son and took their car, then traveled to O'Fallon, Missouri, where he stole a car and began another string of car thefts and attempted abductions. In Wright City, Missouri, on the eastern side of the state, one of the vehicles Jackson had stolen was spotted by a police officer at a gasoline station.

When the officer approached, Jackson fired once with a shotgun, grazing the officer's forehead. Later, authorities found the car abandoned seventy miles outside Wright City. The owner, who had been in the trunk, was shaken but not seriously injured.

Authorities concentrated their manhunt on Wright City and the surrounding area, and dozens of heavily armed officers set up roadblocks and began a search of all buildings, believing Jackson might have become bogged down in the wet, unfamiliar terrain.

Residents of Wright City locked doors and loaded weapons while authorities patrolled outside. The day after Jackson was named to the Most Wanted List, officers received a report that a man matching his description was seen hitchhiking at Lake St. Louis, about twenty miles away, earlier in the day. The hitchhiker was wearing a blue raincoat. One officer remembered seeing a blue raincoat hanging in an abandoned barn near Wright City.

Four officers went to check the barn. As they approached it, they heard a muffled shotgun blast. One hit the ground, and the others ran. Two shots were fired by police at the barn to cover the escape of the remaining officer. Police then began using a bullhorn to try and persuade Jackson to come out. Reporters heard police try to coax him out. Police then lobbed tear gas inside and brought in two helicopters with searchlights. But a search found Jackson's body in a loft; he had killed himself with his gun.

"We can finally unload our shotguns," said one Wright City resident after the discovery. "It's like having a load of bricks lifted off your shoulder."

It was later discovered that an O'Fallon man who had been thought to have died in a one-car automobile accident was actually a victim of Jackson, having been shot in the head when Jackson either mistook the car for that of the police or tried to commandeer it.

Jackson's family members said they had tried to have him institutionalized just before his spree.

No. 409
DAVID JAMES ROBERTS

First Most Wanted Listing:
April 27, 1987
Apprehended:
February 11, 1988

The FBI credited the Fox television network's first broadcast of their "America's Most Wanted" program with a part in the arrest of convicted murderer David Roberts.

Roberts escaped from prison in 1986 while returning from a medical facility in Indianapolis where he had received treatment for numerous stabbing and gunshot wounds, reportedly sustained in a prison riot. On the way back to the prison, Roberts produced a small handgun, handcuffed the two guards, and forced them to accompany him to Hammond, Indiana. The guards later escaped when Roberts stopped to make a telephone call.

At the time of his escape, Roberts had been serving six life sentences, three of which were commuted death sentences. In 1974, Roberts was convicted of murdering a young married couple and their two-year-old daughter. They were killed by a fire he set in their home in Whiteland, Indiana.

He was also convicted in 1974 for the kidnaping and rape of an Indianapolis woman as well as the murder and kidnaping of her six-month-old son. The boy died of exposure after being left in a wooded area overnight. The boy's mother, who had been brutally raped during the night, was found locked in the trunk of her automobile the following day.

The FBI bulletin announcing Roberts's addition to the Most Wanted List said the fugitive had "a small scar on his back near his shoulder blade, and a one-inch scar on his right knee. Roberts reportedly also has numerous additional scars from gunshot wounds, knives, and surgery."

The FBI said Roberts's arrest came after a concerned citizen, spurred by a printed advertisement and the first airing of "America's Most Wanted," aided an intense investigation. Roberts was apprehended by the FBI in Staten Island, New York, without incident.

No. 410
RONALD GLYN TRIPLETT

First Most Wanted Listing:
April 27, 1987
Apprehended:
May 16, 1987

Ronald Triplett, convicted for armed robbery and attempted murder, slipped through the criminal justice system once after escaping from prison. A year later, he wasn't so lucky.

Triplett came to the attention of the FBI after he escaped from the Southern Michigan Prison in Jackson, Michigan, on June 14, 1984. At the time of his escape, Triplett was serving a lengthy sentence for the 1978 robbery of a restaurant in Trenton, Michigan, during which a female employee was shot and wounded with a .45 caliber automatic handgun.

In May 1986 Triplett also allegedly abducted a young couple in Bernalillo County, New Mexico. He threatened them with a small handgun, forced the man into the trunk of a car, then raped the woman. Just over a week later, Triplett, who was reportedly carrying a .25 caliber automatic handgun, forced a woman to accompany him in his truck to a remote area. When he reportedly had begun to rape her, local police officers appeared at the scene and, following a high-speed chase, arrested him.

Triplett, who had been using an alias, posted a $100,000 cash bond and then failed to appear at his arraignment. The FBI description of the fugitive said he was reportedly an avid amateur hockey and softball player and had worked as an assembly line worker, spray painter, health club manager, landscaper, and mechanic.

In May 1987 Triplett was arrested without incident in Tempe, Arizona.

No. 413
DARREN DEE O'NEALL

First Most Wanted Listing:
June 25, 1987
Apprehended:
February 3, 1988

Darren O'Neall was named as a suspect in a violent crime spree in which two young women were murdered and another disappeared. He was eventually discovered in a Louisiana prison, having been arrested several months earlier on a car theft warrant.

O'Neall had been charged with killing a twenty-one-year-old woman, whose skeletal remains and clothing were discovered on May 25, 1987, near Greenwater, Washington. He was also sought in the disappearance of a twenty-nine-year-old Washington woman, who had been missing since April 29, 1987, and he was a suspect in the strangulation murder of a twenty-two-year-old Idaho woman, whose partially decomposed body was discovered June 13, 1987, near La Grande, Oregon.

The FBI bulletin said: "O'Neall, described as a chain smoker and a pathological liar, has often been known to obtain rides from cross-country truckers and to reside at city missions and flop houses. He is reportedly an avid reader of western novels by Louis L'Amour and has taken some of his aliases from characters in those novels."

Among O'Neall's aliases were Mike James Johnson, Jerry Zebulan, Macranahan, Zebulan J. Macranahan, Larry Sackett, Buppy, and Zeb.

After he was arrested on December 30, 1987, in Lakeland, Florida, on a Louisiana car theft warrant, O'Neall gave the name John Mayeaux. He was extradited through normal procedures to Louisiana, where authorities turned up his true identity through a routine fingerprint check.

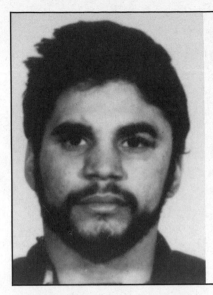

No. 416
PEDRO LUIS ESTRADA

First Most Wanted Listing:
April 15, 1988
Apprehended:
October 1, 1989

Another tip of the hat went to the "America's Most Wanted" television program after FBI agents in Harrisburg, Pennsylvania, captured Pedro Estrada, who was wanted in connection with three murders.

Twenty-five-year-old Estrada was said by federal agents to be a drug gang enforcer, wanted by the New York City Police Department in connection with three killings, in two of which the victims were bound and then shot in the throat.

The FBI said that it received several tips about Estrada after a program televised in 1988. A tip received only days before the arrest helped lead to Estrada's home. He was arrested without a struggle, according to authorities.

No. 418
JACK DARRELL FARMER

First Most Wanted Listing:
May 29, 1988
Apprehended:
June 1, 1988

Jack Farmer, a convicted drug dealer wanted for racketeering activities—including two murders—was arrested after a viewer of the "America's Most Wanted" program recognized his picture.

Farmer was believed to be the ringleader of a Chicago organization known as the Little Mafia. Indicted for racketeering activity—including the two murders, drug trafficking, extortion, several robberies, home invasions, false credit transactions, and threatening to harm a witness who was to testify against him in a trial—Farmer was denied bail and held pending trial.

In April 1987 he was released to his lawyer's custody for day visits to prepare for the upcoming trial. During one of these visits, Farmer, assisted by his wife, tied and gagged the lawyer and escaped.

FBI Director William S. Sessions appeared on the TV program in May 1988 and announced that Farmer and two other men had been named to the Most Wanted List. In response to the program, FBI agents in Miami received information from a citizen that Farmer appeared to be identical to Robert J. Niewiadomski, who was working for a supermarket chain in Deerfield Beach, Florida, and living in Lantana, Florida.

Farmer's wife, Pamela, was arrested first, after she left a Lantana residence. A few minutes later, Farmer bolted from the house but was quickly apprehended. Pamela Farmer was wanted for aiding her husband's escape and bond default.

No. 426
COSTABILE "GUS" FARACE

First Most Wanted Listing:
March 17, 1989
Apprehended:
November 17, 1989

Four shots that killed a federal drug enforcement agent on February 28, 1989, echoed not only in the deserted New York neighborhood where the crime occurred, but throughout Washington, D.C., and the entire country, according to President George Bush.

Two weeks after the murder, President Bush paid a visit to the widow and two sons of the Drug Enforcement Administration agent who had died, and called for the death penalty for those who murder a federal officer.

"Drug dealers need to understand a simple fact," President Bush said. "You shoot a cop, and you will be severely punished, fast. And if I had my way, I'd say with your life."

Within hours of the murder, federal authorities named Costabile "Gus" Farace, a Staten Island, New York, resident, as a suspect. He was described as having been linked to both drug trafficking and organized crime.

The DEA agent, Everett Hatcher, was to have met Farace at a desolate clearing in Staten Island's Rossville section, for a meeting that Hatcher had told fellow agents would not be dangerous. "No dope, no money, just talk," Hatcher had told another agent before the meeting, to which he went unarmed.

Still, Hatcher was watched by four other DEA agents and a member of the FBI. But shortly after 9:00 P.M., agents were observing Hatcher in his sedan at the side of a road when a light-colored van pulled up. Farace was presumed to be the driver of the van, according to newspaper stories that were published after the murder.

The two vehicles then drove off. Agents followed but soon lost radio contact with Hatcher—who had a transmitter on him—and lost sight of him in the heavy traffic. At 10:15 P.M. the agents drove back to the starting point and found Hatcher slumped over the steering wheel of his car, dead. One of four shots had hit Hatcher in the head.

In the days that followed, Robert Stutman, the chief of the DEA's New York office, said he had dropped all pending investigations and begun the largest manhunt in years. "We are going to get him," he vowed.

The agency said that Hatcher, forty-six at the time, was working the case undercover and that he was trying to infiltrate a mob-run cocaine ring.

Several weeks later, the FBI added Farace to the Most Wanted List and said that a joint FBI/DEA nationwide manhunt was under way to find him.

Farace was described as approximately twenty-nine to thirty years of age, with a six-foot–two-inch, 220-pound "muscular" frame, and brown hair. His occupation was listed as "grocery man." He was said to have tattoos of a rose with "Mom and Dad" on his upper left arm, a girl on the lower calf of his right leg, and a butterfly on his stomach.

Farace had been paroled from a state prison in 1988 after serving eight years of a seven- to twenty-one-year term for first-degree manslaughter. He was charged in March with interstate flight to avoid confinement for manslaughter and for a parole violation.

The bureau said that "Farace should be considered armed and extremely dangerous in view of prior conviction for manslaughter and also in view of the nature of the suspected crime."

On November 17, 1989, Farace died before he could be apprehended, killed in a blaze of bullets on a Brooklyn street in what authorities described as an apparent execution by local organized-crime groups.

The 1980s
Rogues' Gallery

No. 373
RONALD TURNEY WILLIAMS

First Most Wanted Listing:
April 16, 1980
Apprehended:
June 8, 1981

Williams had a long record of convictions, including murder, and an equally lengthy list of prison escapes. On November 7, 1979, he added another escape—and allegedly another murder—to his record. On that day Williams, who was serving a life term for the 1975 slaying of a West Virginia police officer, escaped along with fourteen other inmates from the Moundsville State Penitentiary in West Virginia. During the escape the convicts allegedly commandeered a passing vehicle and fatally shot the driver, an off-duty West Virginia state trooper. Williams was charged with murder in connection with the incident. He was arrested in New York City when agents, acting on a tip, approached him in the lobby of a Manhattan hotel. Williams drew a gun, but agents shot him on the spot.

No. 376
GILBERT EUGENE EVERETT

First Most Wanted Listing:
May 13, 1981
Apprehended:
August 12, 1985

Wanted for a series of armed bank robberies and auto thefts, Everett escaped from a Tennessee jail in 1980. He was known to carry a gun strapped to his leg, and another revolver in a hollowed-out book.

No. 381
CHARLES EDWARD WATSON

First Most Wanted Listing:
October 22, 1982
Apprehended:
October 25, 1983

Convicted in the 1975 shotgun murder of a Maryland state trooper and sentenced to life plus ninety-five years, Watson had served six years before he escaped from the Patuxent Correctional Institution in Maryland. He was arrested without incident as he left his residence in Slatington, Pennsylvania.

No. 383
GEORGE CLARENCE BRIDGETTE

First Most Wanted Listing:
January 13, 1984
Apprehended:
January 30, 1984

Bridgette, previously convicted of armed robbery, parole violation, forgery, and auto theft, was sought in connection with the drug-related murders of three adults and one child. In September 1977 he and two accomplices reportedly entered a Long Beach, California, residence, where they allegedly shot five people, killing four. He was arrested in Miami, Florida, only weeks after he was named to the Most Wanted List. His arrest occurred without incident.

No. 389
CLEVELAND MCKINLEY DAVIS

First Most Wanted Listing:
June 15, 1984
Apprehended:
October 24, 1984

A karate expert, Davis was sought in connection with the drug-related murder of a Virginia Beach, Virginia, man who was shot in the head in his home. Davis, previously convicted of armed robbery, possession of a sawed-off shotgun (which he wore on a sling under his jacket), malicious assault, assault, coercion and unlawful imprisonment, burglary, breaking and entering, escape, and parole violation, was arrested without incident in New York City.

No. 391
LOHMAN RAY MAYS

First Most Wanted Listing:
February 15, 1985
Apprehended:
September 23, 1985

Mays, who had been serving a life sentence as a habitual criminal, was sought in connection with his escape from a Tennessee prison on July 1, 1984.

No. 398
BRIAN PATRICK MALVERTY

First Most Wanted Listing:
March 28, 1986
Apprehended:
April 7, 1986

A reported drug dealer, Malverty was sought in connection with the murder of two men in Atlanta, Georgia. The men were shot in the head, chest, and back. Subsequent to the shooting, gasoline was poured over the victims' bodies and set on fire.

No. 401
DONALD KEITH WILLIAMS

First Most Wanted Listing:
July 18, 1986
Apprehended:
August 20, 1986

Williams, fifty-seven when he was added to the Most Wanted List, was wanted in connection with at least thirty bank robberies throughout six states. He had been dubbed the Veil Bandit because he reportedly wore a baseball cap with a cloth over the visor to conceal his features. He had numerous prior convictions for armed robbery, forgery, and burglary, and was reported to have worn protective body armor. He was apprehended without incident in Los Angeles by FBI agents. Williams was armed with a .22 caliber automatic pistol and a starter pistol at the time of his arrest.

No. 404
JAMES WESLEY DYESS

First Most Wanted Listing:
September 29, 1986
Apprehended:
March 16, 1988

Dyess, who had previously been convicted of burglary, larceny, theft, and grand larceny, was wanted in connection with the April 26, 1986, burglary of a Clarke County, Mississippi, residence and the subsequent murders of its two occupants with a .22 caliber revolver. On the day preceding the killings, Dyess escaped from the Clarke County Jail while awaiting transfer to the Mississippi State Penitentiary to serve a seven-year sentence for burglary and habitual criminal convictions. He was arrested by members of the Los Angeles Police Department while driving a vehicle that had been reported stolen. He was unarmed and offered no resistance, according to arrest records.

No. 405
DANNY MICHAEL WEEKS

First Most Wanted Listing:
September 29, 1986
Apprehended:
March 20, 1988

Weeks, serving a life sentence for murder and armed robbery, escaped with two other inmates from the Louisiana State Penitentiary on August 23, 1986. In the period following his escape, he allegedly kidnaped two women in separate instances. Both were later released unharmed. Weeks also allegedly robbed a savings and loan association in San Antonio, Texas, and a bank in Tucson, Arizona.

No. 407
THOMAS GEORGE HARRELSON

First Most Wanted Listing:
November 28, 1986
Apprehended:
February 9, 1987

Harrelson was sought in connection with the armed robbery of a bank in Rossville, Illinois, during which he and an unidentified associate, who carried a 9mm handgun, reportedly stole over $50,000. During an ensuing chase, Harrelson and his companion allegedly stopped their vehicle and fired at a pursuing police officer with the handgun and a 12-gauge shotgun. The officer was not harmed.

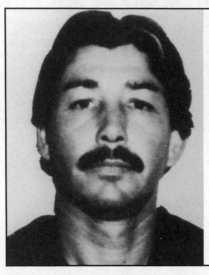

No. 408
ROBERT ALAN LITCHFIELD

First Most Wanted Listing:
January 20, 1987
Apprehended:
May 20, 1987

Litchfield was sought in connection with stealing over $190,000 in a series of three bank robberies in Georgia, Florida, and Michigan. He took hostages, used handguns, and issued bomb threats, and he arrived at all three banks in a taxi, telling the driver to wait for him while he conducted "business transactions." He returned to the taxi and immediately drove off following each of the robberies.

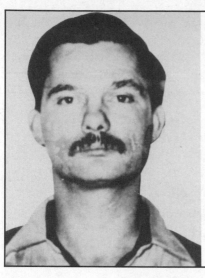

No. 414
LOUIS RAY BEAM, JR.

First Most Wanted Listing:
July 14, 1987
Apprehended:
November 6, 1987

Beam, said by the FBI to be a known associate of members of the right-wing, white-supremacist Aryan Nation movement, was wanted for allegedly conspiring to overthrow the US government by force.

No. 417
JOHN EDWARD STEVENS

First Most Wanted Listing:
May 29, 1988
Apprehended:
November 30, 1988

Stevens was a suspect in twenty-two bank robberies throughout eight states; a total of approximately $500,000 was stolen. Stevens reportedly wore a mask, pulled a handgun, and announced a holdup. He then became loud and abusive, sometimes threatening to shoot bank personnel, and vaulted over the counter to empty the cash drawers himself. He was believed to be skilled in creating fictitious identities and to have gloated that he was smarter than anyone in law enforcement.

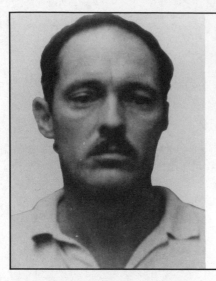

No. 419
ROGER LEE JONES

First Most Wanted Listing:
May 29, 1988
Apprehended:
March 4, 1989

Jones was arrested and charged with performing and videotaping sexual acts with three children. After posting bond, he failed to appear for his trial in November 1986. The FBI said that Jones allegedly endeared himself to neighborhood children, then lured them into increasingly intimate levels of sexual abuse.

No. 420
TERRY LEE JOHNSON

First Most Wanted Listing:
June 12, 1988
Apprehended:
September 8, 1988

Johnson was sought after a daring escape from an Alabama prison in 1986. He had been convicted of a 1976 murder in which he shot a farmer at close range with a high-powered rifle after the man denied him permission to hunt on his property. Johnson was an ex-marine who reportedly was adept at wilderness living.

No. 421
STANLEY FAISON

First Most Wanted Listing:
November 27, 1988
Apprehended:
December 24, 1988

Faison was wanted for allegedly beating a woman with a tire iron until she was unconscious, then waiting for her boyfriend to return and attacking him with the tire iron. Faison then allegedly stabbed the man to death with a butcher knife.

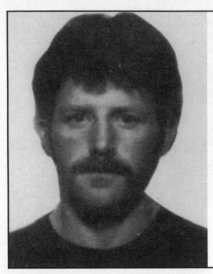

No. 422
STEVEN RAY STOUT

First Most Wanted Listing:
November 27, 1988
Apprehended:
December 6, 1988

Stout was wanted for allegedly killing his former mother-in-law and her nineteen-year-old daughter in West Valley City, Utah. Officials believed that Stout entered the victims' trailer, beat the daughter with a hammer, and stabbed her two times in the chest. He then allegedly waited for the other woman to return home, brutally beat and stabbed her to death, put both bodies in a bedroom, and escaped.

The Current Ten Most Wanted List

No. 366
LEO JOSEPH KOURY

First Most Wanted Listing:
April 20, 1979
Still At Large

No. 375
DONALD EUGENE WEBB

First Most Wanted Listing:
May 4, 1981
Still At Large

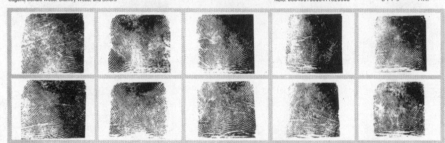

INTERSTATE FLIGHT - MURDER; ATTEMPTED BURGLARY

Entered NCIC

I.O. 4873
Rev. 12-4-86

WANTED BY FBI

DONALD EUGENE WEBB

FBI No. 4 513 086

ALIASES: A.D. Baker, Donald Eugene Perkins (True Name), Donald Eugene Pierce, Stanley J. Pierce, John S. Portas, Stanley John Portas, Bev Webb, Eugene Bevlin Webb, Eugene Donald Webb, Stanley Webb, and others

NCIC: 080406130804TT020906

8S1UⅢ8 Ref: T T U
S1 T Ⅱ   TRR

Photographs taken 1979

Donald E Webb

DESCRIPTION

DATE OF BIRTH: July 14, 1931
PLACE OF BIRTH: Oklahoma City, Oklahoma
HEIGHT: 5'9"
WEIGHT: 165 pounds
BUILD: medium
HAIR: gray-brown
EYES: brown
COMPLEXION: medium
RACE: White
NATIONALITY: American
OCCUPATIONS: butcher, car salesman, jewelry salesman, real estate salesman, restaurant manager, vending machine repairman
SOCIAL SECURITY NUMBER USED: 462-48-0452
SCARS AND MARKS: allegedly has small scar on right cheek and right forearm; tattoos: allegedly "DON" on web of right hand, "ANN" on chest.
REMARKS: Webb, who is considered a career criminal and master of assumed identities, specializes in the burglary of jewelry stores. Reportedly allergic to penicillin, loves dogs, is a flashy dresser, and big tipper.

CRIMINAL RECORD

Webb has been convicted of burglary, possession of counterfeit money, possession of weapon, burglary tools and dangerous instrument, breaking and entering with intent to commit larceny, armed bank robbery and auto larceny.

CAUTION

WEBB IS BEING SOUGHT IN CONNECTION WITH THE MURDER OF A POLICE CHIEF WHO WAS SHOT TWICE AT CLOSE RANGE AFTER BEING BRUTALLY BEATEN ABOUT THE HEAD AND FACE WITH A BLUNT INSTRUMENT. CONSIDER WEBB ARMED AND EXTREMELY DANGEROUS, AND AN ESCAPE RISK.

Federal warrants were issued on December 31, 1980, at Pittsburgh, Pennsylvania, and on December 14, 1979, at Albany, New York, charging Webb with Unlawful Interstate Flight to Avoid Prosecution for the crimes of Murder and Attempted Burglary (Title 18, U.S. Code, Section 1073), respectively.

IF YOU HAVE INFORMATION CONCERNING THIS PERSON, PLEASE CONTACT YOUR LOCAL FBI OFFICE. TELEPHONE NUMBERS AND ADDRESSES OF ALL FBI OFFICES LISTED ON BACK.

Identification Order 4873
Revised December 4, 1986

William H. Webster
Director
Federal Bureau of Investigation
Washington, D.C. 20535

No. 386
VICTOR MANUEL GERENA

First Most Wanted Listing:
May 14, 1984
Still At Large

BANK ROBBERY, INTERSTATE FLIGHT - ARMED ROBBERY, THEFT FROM INTERSTATE SHIPMENT

Entered NCIC
I.O. 4946
10-6-83

WANTED BY FBI

VICTOR MANUEL GERENA

FBI No. 134 852 CA2

ALIASES: Victor Ortiz, Victor M. Gerena Ortiz, Victor Manuel Gerena Ortiz

NCIC: POTTTT1016DIAA032212

10 0 5 Tt 16 Ref: 13
I 17 A   17

REWARD: A PRIVATE COMPANY HAS OFFERED UP TO A $250,000 REWARD FOR RECOVERY OF THE MONEY AND $100,000 REWARD FOR INFORMATION LEADING TO THE ARREST AND CONVICTION OF VICTOR MANUEL GERENA.

Photograph taken 1982

Photograph taken 1983

Victor Manuel Gerena

DESCRIPTION
AGE: 25, born June 24, 1958, New York, New York
HEIGHT: 5'6" to 5'7"   EYES: green
WEIGHT: 160 to 169 pounds   COMPLEXION: dark/medium
BUILD: medium - stocky   RACE: white
HAIR: brown   NATIONALITY: American (Puerto Rican descent)
OCCUPATIONS: machinist, security guard
SCARS AND MARKS: one-inch scar on right shoulder blade; mole on right shoulder blade
REMARKS: customarily wears light mustache; noticeably green eyes
SOCIAL SECURITY NUMBER USED: 046-54-2581

CAUTION
GERENA IS BEING SOUGHT IN CONNECTION WITH THE ARMED ROBBERY OF APPROXIMATELY $7 MILLION FROM A SECURITY COMPANY. HE TOOK TWO SECURITY EMPLOYEES HOSTAGE AT GUNPOINT, HANDCUFFED, BOUND AND INJECTED THEM WITH AN UNKNOWN SUBSTANCE IN ORDER TO FURTHER DISABLE THEM. GERENA IS BELIEVED TO BE IN POSSESSION OF A .38-CALIBER SMITH AND WESSON REVOLVER AND SHOULD BE CONSIDERED ARMED AND DANGEROUS.

A Federal warrant was issued on September 13, 1983, at Hartford, Connecticut, charging Gerena with the crimes of bank robbery, unlawful interstate flight to avoid prosecution for armed robbery, and theft from interstate shipment (Title 18, U.S. Code, Sections 2113 (a) (d), 1073 and 659).

IF YOU HAVE INFORMATION CONCERNING THIS PERSON, PLEASE CONTACT YOUR LOCAL FBI OFFICE. TELEPHONE NUMBERS AND ADDRESSES OF ALL FBI OFFICES LISTED ON BACK.

Identification Order 4946
October 6, 1983

William H. Webster
Director
Federal Bureau of Investigation
Washington, D. C. 20535

No. 411
CLAUDE DANIEL MARKS

First Most Wanted Listing:
May 22, 1987
Still At Large

CONSPIRACY TO VIOLATE PRISON ESCAPE, DAMAGE AND DESTRUCTION OF GOVERNMENT PROPERTY, RECEIPT AND TRANSPORTATION OF EXPLOSIVES, INTERSTATE TRAVEL TO PROMOTE CRIMINAL ACTIVITY, POSSESSION OF UNREGISTERED FIREARMS

Entered NCIC
I.O. 5034
4-30-87

WANTED BY FBI
CLAUDE DANIEL MARKS

FBI No. 83 249 FA4

ALIASES: Claudio Daniel Makowski (True Name), John Chester Clark, Edward Cole, Charles Everett, Michael Hamlin, C. Henley, Dale Allen Martin, Tony McCormick, Michael Prentiss, Brian Wilcox, and others

Photographs taken 1985

DESCRIPTION

DATES OF BIRTH USED: December 31, 1949 (true date of birth) February 11, 1944; November 1, 1945; June 8, 1950; February 6, 1951; June 26, 1951; March 26, 1955
PLACE OF BIRTH: Buenos Aires, Argentina
HEIGHT: 6'
EYES: brown
WEIGHT: 190 pounds
COMPLEXION: medium
BUILD: heavy
RACE: white
HAIR: brown
NATIONALITY: American
SCARS AND MARKS: mole on neck
OCCUPATIONS: fast food cook, radio announcer, auto mechanic, printer
REMARKS: Marks is a martial arts enthusiast and allegedly is knowledgeable of electronics and automobile maintenance, weapons, explosives, and reloading procedures. Reportedly speaks fluent Spanish. Wears contact lenses or glasses. Marks may be accompanied by Donna Jean Willmott, FBI Identification Order 5035, WHO IS ALSO WANTED BY LAW ENFORCEMENT AUTHORITIES.
SOCIAL SECURITY NUMBERS USED: 551-80-8393; 129-62-4064; 287-03-2916; 299-05-3771; 520-82-1220; 568-75-8212; 601-34-2856; 120-68-4648; 547-67-2897; 608-98-2730; 561-67-2823; 692-42-9631; 556-31-3362; 015-65-0510; 525-36-4427

A Federal warrant was issued on December 12, 1986 at Chicago, Illinois, charging Marks with violation of Title 18, U.S. Code, Section 371 (Conspiracy) to violate; Title 18, U.S. Code, Section 751 (a), 752 (a) (Prison Escape); Title 18, U.S. Code, Section 844 (f) (Damage and Destruction of Government Property by means of Fire or Explosives); Title 18, U.S. Code, Section 844 (d) (Receipt and Transportation of Explosives); Title 18, U.S. Code, Section 1952 (a)(3) (Interstate Travel to Promote Criminal Activity); and Title 26, U.S. Code, Section 5861(d) (Possession of Unregistered Firearms).

CAUTION

MARKS HAS BEEN TRAINED IN THE MARTIAL ARTS AND HAS BEEN KNOWN TO BE IN POSSESSION OF EXPLOSIVES AND SHOULD BE CONSIDERED ARMED AND DANGEROUS.

IF YOU HAVE INFORMATION CONCERNING THIS PERSON, PLEASE CONTACT YOUR LOCAL FBI OFFICE. TELEPHONE NUMBERS AND ADDRESSES OF ALL FBI OFFICES LISTED ON BACK.

Identification Order 5034
April 30, 1987

William H. Webster
Director
Federal Bureau of Investigation
Washington, D.C. 20535

No. 412
DONNA JEAN WILLMOTT

First Most Wanted Listing:
May 22, 1987
Still At Large

CONSPIRACY TO VIOLATE PRISON ESCAPE, DAMAGE AND DESTRUCTION OF GOVERNMENT PROPERTY, RECEIPT AND TRANSPORTATION OF EXPLOSIVES, INTERSTATE TRAVEL TO PROMOTE CRIMINAL ACTIVITY, POSSESSION OF UNREGISTERED FIREARMS

Entered NCIC
I.O. 5035
4-30-87

WANTED BY FBI
DONNA JEAN WILLMOTT

FBI No. 867 585 EA5

ALIASES: J. Billings, Marcie Garber, Marcia Gardner, Jean Gill, Dona J. Krupnick, Donna J. Willmott, Donna Jean Willmot, Donna Wilmiet, Donna Jean Willmott, Terry Young, and others

NCIC: 121109PM12AA1009CH10

12 9 U OIM 12
2a U OI I

Photographs taken 1985

Donna J. Willmott

DESCRIPTION
DATES OF BIRTH USED: June 30, 1950 (true date of birth)
December 15, 1956
PLACE OF BIRTH: Akron, Ohio
HEIGHT: 5'   EYES: brown
WEIGHT: 105 pounds   COMPLEXION: ruddy
BUILD: small   RACE: white
HAIR: brown (dyed blonde)   NATIONALITY: American
OCCUPATIONS: hospital technician, nurse, lab technician, acupuncturist, housekeeper
REMARKS: Willmott is known to use false identification and change appearance utilizing wigs and/or dyed hair. Wears corrective lenses. Willmott has reportedly taken martial arts courses. Willmott may be accompanied by Claude Daniel Marks, FBI Identification Order 5034, WHO IS ALSO WANTED BY LAW ENFORCEMENT AUTHORITIES.
SOCIAL SECURITY NUMBERS USED: 270-50-0840; 360-42-8763; 360-42-8736; 567-67-9133; 390-18-4818

CAUTION
WILLMOTT HAS REPORTEDLY TAKEN MARTIAL ARTS LESSONS AND HAS BEEN KNOWN TO POSSESS EXPLOSIVES AND A WIDE ARRAY OF WEAPONS AND SHOULD BE CONSIDERED ARMED AND DANGEROUS.

A Federal warrant was issued on December 12, 1986 at Chicago, Illinois, charging Willmott with violation of Title 18, U.S. Code, Section 371 (Conspiracy) to violate; Title 18, U.S. Code, Section 751 (a), 752 (a) (Prison Escape); Title 18, U.S. Code, Section 844 (f) (Damage and Destruction of Government Property by means of Fire or Explosives); Title 18, U.S. Code, Section 844 (d) (Receipt and Transportation of Explosives); Title 18, U.S. Code, Section 1952 (a) (3) (Interstate Travel to Promote Criminal Activity); and Title 26, U.S. Code, Section 5861 (d) (Possession of Unregistered Firearms).

IF YOU HAVE INFORMATION CONCERNING THIS PERSON, PLEASE CONTACT YOUR LOCAL FBI OFFICE. TELEPHONE NUMBERS AND ADDRESSES OF ALL FBI OFFICES LISTED ON BACK.

Identification Order 5035
April 30, 1987

William H. Webster
Director
Federal Bureau of Investigation
Washington, D.C. 20535

No. 423
ARMANDO GARCIA

First Most Wanted Listing:
January 8, 1989
Still At Large

No. 424
MELVIN EDWARD MAYS

First Most Wanted Listing:
February 7, 1989
Still At Large

INTERSTATE TRANSPORTATION OF EXPLOSIVES; CONSPIRACY; RECEIPT AND TRANSPORTATION OF EXPLOSIVES; INTERSTATE TRAVEL TO PROMOTE CRIMINAL ACTIVITY; POSSESSION OF UNREGISTERED FIREARMS

Entered
NCIC
I.O 5047
7-29-87

WANTED BY FBI

MELVIN EDWARD MAYS

FBI No. 5 830 AA4

Aliases: Melvin Mays, Melvin E. Mays, "Maumee," "Maumie"

NCIC: 1817091914D0AAQ8PMPI

18 L 6 U OIO 14 Ref: 22
0 2 A IM 2

Photographs taken 1982

DESCRIPTION

DATE OF BIRTH: September 7, 1957
PLACE OF BIRTH: Chicago, Illinois
HEIGHT: 5'9"
WEIGHT: 165 pounds
BUILD: medium
HAIR: black
EYES: brown
COMPLEXION: dark
RACE: black
NATIONALITY: American
SOCIAL SECURITY
NUMBER USED: 354-56-8017
REMARKS: He may have a beard and moustache. He is missing several upper left front teeth and stutters when he speaks.

CRIMINAL RECORD

Mays has been convicted of obstructing a police officer.

CAUTION

MAYS IS BEING SOUGHT IN CONNECTION WITH THE PURCHASE OF AN EXPLOSIVE DEVICE. HE IS A KNOWN MEMBER OF A VIOLENT STREET GANG AND IS KNOWN TO POSSESS AUTOMATIC WEAPONS. CONSIDER ARMED AND DANGEROUS AND A NARCOTICS USER.

A Federal warrant was issued on August 5, 1985, at Chicago, Illinois, charging Mays with Interstate Transportation of Explosives (Title 18, U.S. Code, Section 844 (d)). On April 1, 1987, a Federal grand jury at Chicago, Illinois, returned an indictment charging Mays with Conspiracy (Title 18, U.S. Code, Section 371); Receipt and Transportation of Explosives (Title 18, U.S. Code, Section1952 (a) (3)); Interstate Travel to Promote Criminal Activity (Title 26, U.S. Code, Section 5861 (d)); Possession of Unregistered Firearms (Title 26, U.S. Code, Section 5871).

IF YOU HAVE INFORMATION CONCERNING THIS PERSON, PLEASE CONTACT YOUR LOCAL FBI OFFICE. TELEPHONE NUMBERS AND ADDRESSES OF ALL FBI OFFICES LISTED ON BACK.

Identification Order 5047
July 29, 1987

Acting Director
Federal Bureau of Investigation
United States Department of Justice
Washington, D.C. 20535

No. 427
ARTHUR LEE WASHINGTON, JR.

First Most Wanted Listing:
October 18, 1989
Still At Large

WANTED BY THE FBI

INTERSTATE FLIGHT-ATTEMPTED MURDER

ARTHUR LEE WASHINGTON, JR.

DESCRIPTION

Born, November 30, 1949; Place of Birth: Neptune, New Jersey; Height: 6'1"; Weight: 220 pounds; Build: heavy; Hair: black; Eyes: brown; Complexion: medium; Race: Black; Nationality: American; Scars and Marks: scar on right rear of neck, old track marks on both arms, scar on left wrist, scar on right wrist, scar on upper right leg; Occupation: laborer. Remarks: Washington has been associated in the past with militant black prison groups and the Black Liberation Army. Social Security Number Used: 136-40-5847.

CAUTION

WASHINGTON IS BEING SOUGHT IN CONNECTION WITH THE ATTEMPTED MURDER OF A NEW JERSEY STATE TROOPER WHEREIN A .45 CALIBER SEMI-AUTOMATIC HANDGUN WAS USED. CONSIDERED ARMED AND EX-TREMELY DANGEROUS. HE MAY HAVE ACQUIRED IMMUNE DEFICIENCY SYNDROME (AIDS).

FBI/DOJ

No. 429
WARDELL DAVID FORD

First Most Wanted Listing:
December 20, 1989
Still At Large

WANTED BY THE FBI

INTERSTATE FLIGHT - MURDER

WARDELL DAVID FORD

DESCRIPTION

Date of Birth: May 10, 1956; Place of Birth: Detroit, Michigan; Height: 5'9";
Weight: 150 pounds; Build: medium; Hair: black; Eyes: brown; Complexion:
medium; Race: Black; Nationality: American; Occupation: construction laborer;
Remarks: Wears prescription glasses and may be clean shaven; Social Security Number Used: 369-64-7878

CRIMINAL RECORD

Ford has been convicted of armed robbery, fraud and larceny.

CAUTION

FORD IS BEING SOUGHT IN CONNECTION WITH ROBBERY AND SUBSE-
QUENT MURDER OF A PUROLATOR ARMORED CAR SERVICE GUARD.
HE MAY BE ARMED WITH A .22-CALIBER REVOLVER AND SHOULD BE
CONSIDERED ARMED AND DANGEROUS.

FBI/DOJ

No. 430
LESLIE ISBEN ROGGE

First Most Wanted Listing:
January 24, 1990
Still At Large

BANK ROBBERY; INTERSTATE TRANSPORTATION OF STOLEN PROPERTY; FRAUD BY WIRE

Entered NCIC
I.O. 5097
Rev.
10-2-89

WANTED BY FBI
LESLIE ISBEN ROGGE

FBI No. 740 180 D

24 L 9 U OOO 17
    L 2 U OOI

Aliases: J. Carpenter, Rodney William Dickens, Leslie Gibseen, Leslie Isben Moore, Robert Charles Nelson, Fred Pratts, Wally Preston, Leslie Gibson Rogle, Donald Clark Rose, Donald King Williams, and others

NCIC: 242326PO17171720PI18

Photographs Taken 1989

DESCRIPTION
Dates of Birth Used: March 8, 1940 (true date of birth)
June 15, 1942
Place of Birth: Seattle, Washington
Height: 5'11"   **Eyes:** blue
Weight: 160 pounds   **Complexion:** medium
Build: medium   **Race:** White
Hair: brown (greying) **Nationality:** American
Scars and Marks and Tattoos: Sea horse on left shoulder, Eagle on right shoulder, Dragon on left shoulder, Devil with word "Les" on right forearm, and may also have a peacock on one arm.
Occupations: carpenter, expert recreational sailor, machinist
Remarks: Rogge may have a police scanner in his possession. He wears Foster Grant dark wire-rimmed glasses. He has previously owned and operated large sailboats and has sailed extensively off the coast of Mexico. He may also be in possession of a retired Navy identification card. He may be traveling with his wife, Judy Kay Wilson, date of birth, June 28, 1955, Height 5' 7", 135 pounds, brown eyes, brown hair, Social Security Number Used: 437-70-5123. WILSON IS ALSO WANTED BY LAW ENFORCEMENT AUTHORITIES.
Social Security Numbers Used: 538-38-3421; 454-08-2573; 531-38-3241; 538-38-3241

CRIMINAL RECORD
Rogge has been convicted of Armed Bank Robbery, Robbery, Grand Larceny, Ex-Convict in Possession of a Firearm, and Failure to Appear.

A Federal warrant was issued on April 14, 1986, at Harrison, Arkansas, charging Rogge with Bank Robbery (Title 18, U.S. Code, Section 2113 (a)). Federal warrants were also issued on March 3, 1989, at Charleston, South Carolina, charging Rogge with Interstate Transportation of Stolen Property (Title 18, U.S. Code, Section 2314) and Fraud by Wire (Title 18, U.S. Code, Section 1343); and August 28, 1989, at Greensboro, North Carolina, charging Rogge with Bank Robbery (Title 18, U.S. Code, Section 2113 (a) and 924 (c)). Rogge is also wanted in Moscow, Idaho, as an Escaped Federal Prisoner.

IF YOU HAVE ANY INFORMATION CONCERNING THIS PERSON, PLEASE CONTACT YOUR LOCAL FBI OFFICE. TELEPHONE NUMBERS AND ADDRESSES OF ALL FBI OFFICES LISTED ON BACK.

Identification Order 5097
Revised October 2, 1989

CAUTION
ROGGE, AN ESCAPEE FROM CUSTODY, IS BEING SOUGHT FOR A SERIES OF BANK ROBBERIES IN WHICH A HANDGUN WAS USED. CONSIDER ARMED AND EXTREMELY DANGEROUS AND AN ESCAPE RISK.

DIRECTOR
FEDERAL BUREAU OF INVESTIGATION
WASHINGTON, D.C. 20535

Afterword

On March 14, 1990, the Most Wanted program celebrated its fortieth anniversary. It's not likely, though, that many criminals joined in the festivities, for the Most Wanted List has a phenomenal success rate—over 90 percent of all Most Wanted fugitives have been apprehended.

Today's hardened criminals probably feel the same way about the FBI as Walter James Wilkinson did. Wilkinson was the alleged leader of a New York State bandit gang in the 1950s. When captured at the Fox Hill Country Club in Los Angeles, where he was working as a busboy, Wilkinson said, "It didn't take you long—I know that is the way you work."

Another 1950s Most Wanted fugitive was reported to have said after his apprehension, "You just have to retire after you make the big list—you can't go around the country doing crazy things anymore once you're on it."

A great deal of the Most Wanted program's success, of course, must be attributed to the FBI itself and to the cooperation of law enforcement officials throughout the country.

No less a "partner" in the Most Wanted program is the average American citizen. The Bureau itself points to more than 120 Most Wanted fugitives who were apprehended as a result of citizen involvement. For the most part, these citizens have remained anonymous, with the Bureau stating that it did not want to endanger their safety.

Throughout the writing and publication of *Most Wanted,* criminals have not ceased their activities. Though more than a few criticisms have been aimed at the Most Wanted program and though the FBI has changed its priorities for fugitive apprehension, there is no doubt that the Most Wanted List will continue. ("The Current Ten Most Wanted List" in the previous chapter represents the state of the Most Wanted List as close to the time of publication as printing requirements allowed. Any subsequent editions will reflect future FBI apprehensions and additions.)

As criminal techniques become more and more sophisticated and the FBI's own methods keep pace, the average American citizen will continue to play a key role in the investigative process.

Most Wanted posters tacked on post office walls may become dusty, but television programs such as "America's Most Wanted" will keep the faces of fugitives in the public eye.

What should you do if you recognize a Most Wanted fugitive? The FBI suggests that you call the nearest Bureau office—listed at the back of this book or in your local telephone directory—or the local police.

Almost without exception, Most Wanted fugitives are considered to be "armed and extremely dangerous." A private citizen's biggest help to law officers is in using the telephone to provide the tip, then letting authorities take over.

A
Chronological Listing
of the FBI's
"Ten Most Wanted
Fugitives"

MAY 14, 1950 to the PRESENT

	NAME	DATE ADDED	DATE APPREHENDED
1.	Thomas J. Holden	3/14/50	6/23/51
2.	Morley V. King	3/15/50	10/31/51
3.	William R. Nesbit	3/16/50	3/18/50
4.	Henry R. Mitchell	3/17/50	7/18/58
5.	Omar A. Pinson	3/18/50	8/28/50
6.	Lee Emory Downs	3/20/50	4/7/50
7.	Orba Elmer Jackson	3/21/50	3/22/50
8.	Glen Roy Wright	3/22/50	6/23/50
9.	Henry Harland Shelton	3/23/50	6/23/50
10.	Morris Guralnick	3/24/50	12/15/50
11.	William F. Sutton	3/20/50	2/18/52
12.	Stephen W. Davenport	4/4/50	5/5/50
13.	Henry Clay Tollett	4/11/50	6/3/51
14.	Frederick J. Tenuto	5/24/50	3/9/64
15.	Thomas Kling	7/17/50	2/20/52
16.	Meyer Dembin	9/5/50	11/26/51
17.	Courtney T. Taylor	1/8/51	2/16/51
18.	Joseph F. Bent, Jr.	1/9/51	8/29/52
19.	Harry H. Burton	3/9/51	2/7/52
20.	Joseph Cato (surrendered before release date)	6/27/51	6/21/51
21.	Anthony Brancato	6/27/51	6/29/51
22.	Frederick E. Peters	7/2/51	1/15/52
23.	Ernest Tait	7/11/51	7/12/51
24.	Ollie Gene Embry	7/25/51	8/5/51
25.	Giachino A. Baccollo	8/20/51	12/10/51
26.	Raymond E. Young	11/12/51	11/16/51
27.	John Thomas Hill	12/10/51	8/16/52
28.	George Arthur Heroux	12/19/51	7/25/52
29.	Sydney Gordon Martin	1/7/52	11/27/53
30.	Gerhard Arthur Puff	1/28/52	7/26/52
31.	Thomas Edward Young	2/21/52	9/23/52
32.	Kenneth Lee Maurer	2/27/52	1/8/53
33.	Isaie Aldy Beausoleil	3/3/52	6/25/53
34.	Leonard Joseph Zalutsky	8/5/52	9/8/52
35.	William Merle Martin	8/11/52	8/30/52
36.	James Eddie Diggs	8/27/52	12/14/61
37.	Nick George Montos	9/8/52	8/23/54
38.	Theodore Richard Byrd, Jr.	9/10/52	8/21/54
39.	Harden Collins Kemper	9/17/52	1/1/53
40.	John Joseph Brennan	10/6/52	1/23/53
41.	Charles Patrick Shue	1/15/53	2/13/53
42.	Lawson David Shirt Butler	1/22/53	4/21/53
43.	Joseph James Brletic	2/9/53	2/10/53
44.	David Dallas Taylor	3/3/53	5/26/53
45.	Perlie Miller	3/4/53	3/5/53
46.	Fred William Bowerman	3/5/53	4/24/53
47.	Robert Benton Mathus	3/16/53	3/19/53
48.	Floyd Allen Hill	3/30/53	4/18/53

NAME	DATE ADDED	DATE APPREHENDED
49. Joseph Levy	5/1/53	4/30/53
50. Arnold Hinson	5/4/53	11/7/53
51. Gordon Lee Cooper	5/11/53	6/11/53
52. Fleet Robert Current	5/18/53	7/12/53
53. Donald Charles Fitterer	6/8/53	6/21/53
54. John Raleigh Cooke	6/22/53	10/20/53
55. Jack Gordon White	7/6/53	8/27/53
56. Alex Richard Bryant	7/14/53	1/26/54
57. George William Krendich (body located)	7/27/53	10/11/53
58. Lloyd Reed Russel	9/8/53	8/3/54
59. Edwin Sanford Garrison	10/26/53	11/3/53
60. Franklin James Wilson	11/2/53	1/18/54
61. Charles E. Johnson	11/12/53	12/28/53
62. Thomas Jackson Massingale	11/18/53	11/26/53
63. Peter Edward Kenzik	12/7/53	1/26/55
64. Thomas Everett Dickerson	12/10/53	12/21/53
65. Chester Lee Davenport	1/6/54	1/7/54
66. Alex Whitmore	1/11/54	5/10/54
67. Everett Lowell Krueger	1/25/54	2/15/54
68. Apee Hamp Chapman	2/3/54	2/10/54
69. Nelson Robert Duncan	2/8/54	2/21/54
70. Charles Falzone	2/24/54	8/17/55
71. Basil Kingsley Beck	3/1/54	3/3/54
72. James William Lofton	3/16/54	3/17/54
73. Clarence Dye	3/8/54	8/3/55
74. Sterling Groom	4/2/54	4/21/54
75. Raymond Louis Owen Menard	5/3/54	5/5/54
76. John Alfred Hopkins	5/18/54	6/7/54
77. Otto Austin Loel	5/21/54	1/17/55
78. David Daniel Keegan	6/21/54	12/13/63
79. Walter James Wilkinson	8/17/54	1/12/55
80. John Harry Allen	9/7/54	12/21/54
81. George Lester Belew	1/4/55	1/24/55
82. Kenneth Darrell Carpenter	1/31/55	2/4/55
83. Flenow Payne	2/2/55	3/11/88
84. Palmer Julius Morset	2/7/55	3/2/56
85. Patrick Eugene McDermott	2/9/55	7/19/55
86. Garland William Daniels	2/18/55	3/29/55
87. Daniel William O'Connor	4/11/55	12/26/55
88. Jack Harvey Raymond	8/8/55	10/14/55
89. Daniel Abram Everhart	8/17/55	10/9/55
90. Charles Edward Ranels	9/2/55	12/16/56
91. Thurman Arthur Green	10/24/55	2/16/56
92. John Allen Kendrick	11/2/55	12/2/55
93. Joseph James Bagnola	12/19/55	12/30/56
94. Nick George Montos (second time on list)	3/2/56	3/28/56
95. James Ignatius Faherty	3/19/56	5/16/56

	NAME	DATE ADDED	DATE APPREHENDED
96.	Thomas Francis Richardson	4/12/56	5/16/56
97.	Eugene Francis Newman	5/28/56	6/11/65
98.	Carmine DiBiase	5/28/56	8/28/58
99.	Ben Golden McCollum	1/4/57	3/7/58
100.	Alfred James White	1/14/57	1/24/57
101.	Robert L. Green	2/11/57	2/13/57
102.	George Edward Cole	2/25/57	7/6/59
103.	Eugene Russell McCracken	3/26/58	3/27/58
104.	Frank Aubrey Leftwich	4/4/58	4/18/58
105.	Quay Cleon Kilburn	4/16/58	6/2/58
106.	Dominick Scialo	5/9/58	7/27/59
107.	Angelo Luigi Pero	6/16/58	12/2/60
108.	Frederick Grant Dunn	7/29/58	9/18/59
109.	Frank Lawrence Sprenz	9/10/58	4/15/59
110.	David Lynn Thurston	1/8/59	2/6/59
111.	John Thomas Freeman	2/17/59	2/18/59
112.	Edwin Sanford Garrison	3/4/59	9/9/60
113.	Emmett Bernard Kervan	3/29/59	5/13/59
114.	Richard Allan Hunt	5/27/59	6/2/59
115.	Walter Bernard O'Donnell	6/17/59	6/19/59
116.	Billy Owens Williams	7/10/59	3/4/60
117.	James Francis Jenkins	7/21/59	8/12/59
118.	Harry Raymond Pope	8/26/59	9/2/59
119.	James Francis Duffy	8/11/59	8/25/59
120.	Robert Garfield Brown, Jr.	9/9/59	1/11/60
121.	Frederick Anthony Seno	9/24/59	9/24/59
122.	Smith Gerald Hudson	10/7/59	7/31/60
123.	Joseph Lloyd Thomas	10/21/59	12/10/59
124.	Kenneth Ray Lawson	1/4/60	3/20/60
125.	Ted Jacob Rinehart	1/25/60	3/6/60
126.	Charles Clyatt Rogers	3/18/60	5/11/60
127.	Joseph Corbett, Jr.	3/30/60	10/29/60
128.	William Mason	4/6/60	4/27/60
129.	Edward Reiley	5/10/60	5/24/60
130.	Harold Eugene Fields	5/25/60	9/5/60
131.	Richard Peter Wagner	6/23/60	6/25/60
132.	James John Warjac	7/19/60	7/22/60
133.	Ernest Tait	8/16/60	9/10/60
134.	Clarence Leon Raby	8/19/60	8/28/60
135.	Nathaniel Beans	9/12/60	9/30/60
136.	Stanley William Fitzgerald	9/20/60	9/22/60
137.	Donald Leroy Payne	10/6/60	11/26/65
138.	Charles Francis Higgins	10/10/60	10/17/60
139.	Robert William Schultz, Jr.	10/12/60	11/4/60
140.	Merle Lyle Gall	10/17/60	1/18/61
141.	James George Economou	10/31/60	3/22/61
142.	Ray Delano Tate	11/18/60	11/25/60
143.	John B. Everhart	11/22/60	11/6/63
144.	Herbert Hoove Huffman	12/19/60	12/29/60

NAME	DATE ADDED	DATE APPREHENDED
145. Kenneth Eugene Cindle	12/23/60	4/1/61
146. Thomas Viola	1/17/61	3/27/61
147. William Chester Cole	2/2/61	2/6/61
148. William Hughes	3/15/61	8/8/61
149. William Terry Nichols	4/6/61	4/30/62
150. George Martin Bradley, Jr.	4/10/61	5/1/61
151. Philip Alfred Lanormandin	4/17/61	4/17/61
152. Kenneth Holleck Sharp	5/1/61	7/3/61
153. Anthony Vincent Fede	5/22/61	10/28/61
154. Richard Laurence Marquette	6/29/61	6/30/61
155. Robert William Schuette	7/19/61	8/2/61
156. Chester Anderson McGonigal	8/14/61	8/17/61
157. Hugh Bion Morse	8/29/61	10/13/61
158. John Gibson Dillon	9/1/61	3/2/64
159. John Robert Sawyer	10/30/61	11/3/61
160. Edward Wayne Edwards	11/10/61	1/20/62
161. Franklin Eugene Alltop	11/22/61	2/2/62
162. Francis Laverne Brannan	12/27/61	1/17/62
163. Delbert Henry Linaweaver	1/30/62	2/5/62
164. Watson Young, Jr.	2/5/62	2/12/62
165. Lyndal Ray Smith	2/14/62	3/22/62
166. Harry Robert Grove, Jr.	2/19/62	1/26/63
167. Bobby Randell Wilcoxson	2/23/62	11/10/62
168. Albert Frederick Nussbaum	4/2/62	11/4/62
169. Thomas Welton Holland	5/11/62	6/2/62
170. Edward Howard Maps	6/15/62	12/1/62
171. David Stanley Jacubanis	11/21/62	11/29/62
172. John Kinchloe DeJarnette	11/30/62	12/3/62
173. Michael Joseph O'Connor	12/13/62	12/28/62
174. John Lee Taylor	12/14/62	12/20/62
175. Harold Thomas O'Brien (process dismissed)	1/4/63	1/14/65
176. Jerry Clarence Rush	1/14/63	3/25/63
177. Marshall Frank Chrisman	2/7/63	5/21/63
178. Howard Jay Barnard	4/12/63	4/6/64
179. Leroy Ambrosia Frazier	6/4/63	9/12/63
180. Carl Close	9/25/63	9/26/63
181. Thomas Asbury Hadder	10/9/63	1/13/64
182. Alfred Oponowicz	11/27/63	12/23/64
183. Arthur William Couts	12/27/63	1/30/64
184. Jesse James Gilbert	1/27/64	2/26/64
185. Sammie Carl Ammons	2/10/64	5/15/64
186. Frank B. Dumont	3/10/64	4/27/64
187. William Beverly Hughes	3/18/64	4/11/64
188. Quay Cleon Kilburn (second time on list)	3/23/64	6/25/64
189. Joseph Francis Bryan, Jr.	4/14/64	4/28/64
190. John Robert Bailey	4/22/64	5/4/64
191. George Zavada	5/6/64	6/12/64

	NAME	DATE ADDED	DATE APPREHENDED
192.	George Patrick McLaughlin	5/8/64	2/24/65
193.	Chester Collins	5/14/64	3/30/67
194.	Edward Newton Nivens	5/28/64	6/2/64
195.	Lewis Frederick Vasselli	6/15/64	9/1/64
196.	Thomas Edward Galloway	6/24/64	7/17/64
197.	Alson Thomas Wahrlich	7/9/64	10/28/67
198.	Kenneth Malcolm Christiansen	7/27/64	9/8/64
199.	William Hutton Coble	9/11/64	3/1/65
200.	Lloyd Donald Greeson, Jr.	9/18/64	9/23/64
201.	Raymond Lawrence Wyngaard	10/5/64	11/28/64
202.	Norman Belyea Gorham	12/10/64	5/27/65
203.	John William Clouser (process dismissed)	1/7/65	8/1/72
204.	Walter Lee Parman	1/15/65	1/31/65
205.	Gene Thomas Webb	2/11/65	2/12/65
206.	Samuel Jefferson Veney	2/25/65	3/11/65
207.	Carl Veney	3/5/65	3/11/65
208.	Stewart Heien	3/11/65	2/3/66
209.	Arthur Pierce, Jr.	3/24/65	3/25/65
210.	Donald Dean Rainey	3/26/65	6/22/65
211.	Leslie Douglas Ashley	4/6/65	4/23/65
212.	Charles Bryan Harris	5/6/65	6/17/65
213.	William Albert Autur Tahl	6/10/65	11/5/65
214.	Duane Earl Pope	6/11/65	6/11/65
215.	Allan Wade Haugsted	6/24/65	12/23/65
216.	Theodore Matthew Brechtel	6/30/65	8/16/65
217.	Robert Allen Woodford	7/2/65	8/5/65
218.	Warren Cleveland Osborne	8/12/65	9/9/65
219.	Holice Paul Black	8/25/65	12/15/65
220.	Edward Owen Watkins	9/21/65	12/2/65
221.	Joel Singer	11/19/65	12/1/65
222.	James Edward Kennedy	12/8/65	12/23/65
223.	Lawrence John Higgins	12/14/65	1/3/66
224.	Hoyt Bud Cobb	1/6/66	6/6/66
225.	James Robert Bishop	1/10/66	1/21/66
226.	Robert Van Lewing	1/12/66	2/6/67
227.	Carl Ellery Wright	1/14/66	6/20/66
228.	Jessie James Roberts, Jr.	2/3/66	2/8/66
229.	Charles Lorin Gove	2/16/66	2/16/66
230.	Robert Dwayne Owen	2/16/66	3/11/66
231.	Jimmy Lewis Parker	2/25/66	3/4/66
232.	Jack Daniels Sayadoff	3/17/66	3/24/66
233.	Robert Clayton Buick	3/24/66	3/29/66
234.	James Vernon Taylor	4/4/66	4/4/66
235.	Lynwood Irwin Meares	4/11/66	5/2/67
236.	James Robert Ringrose	4/15/66	3/29/67
237.	Walter Leonard Lesczyinski	6/16/66	9/9/66
238.	Donald Roger Smelley	6/30/66	11/7/66
239.	George Ben Edmondson	9/21/66	6/28/67

	NAME	DATE ADDED	DATE APPREHENDED
240.	Everett Leroy Biggs	9/21/66	12/1/66
241.	Gene Robert Jennings	12/15/66	2/14/67
242.	Clarence Wilbert McFarland	12/22/66	4/4/67
243.	Monroe Hickson	2/17/67	1/30/68
244.	Clyde Edward Laws	2/28/67	5/18/67
245.	Charles Edward Ervin	4/13/67	7/25/67
246.	Gordon Dale Ervin	4/13/67	6/7/69
247.	Thomas Franklin Dorman	4/20/67	5/20/67
248.	Jerry Lynn Young	5/12/67	6/15/67
249.	Joseph Leroy Newman	6/2/67	6/29/67
250.	Carmen Raymond Gagliardi	6/9/67	12/23/68
251.	Donald Richard Bussmeyer	6/28/67	8/24/67
252.	Florencio Lopez Mationg	7/1/67	7/16/67
253.	Victor Jerald Bono	7/1/67	7/16/67
254.	Alfred Johnson Cooper, Jr.	7/27/67	9/8/67
255.	John D. Slaton	8/2/67	12/1/67
256.	Jerry Ray James	8/16/67	1/24/68
257.	Richard Paul Anderson	9/7/67	1/19/68
258.	Henry Theodore Young	9/21/67	1/9/68
259.	Donald Eugene Sparks	11/13/67	1/24/68
260.	Zelma Lavone King	12/14/67	1/30/68
261.	Jerry Reece Peacock	12/14/67	3/5/68
262.	Ronald Eugene Storck	1/19/68	2/29/68
263.	Robert Leon McCain	1/31/68	2/23/68
264.	William Garrin Allen II	2/9/68	3/23/68
265.	Charles Lee Herron	2/9/68	6/18/86
266.	Leonard Daniel Spears	2/13/68	3/2/68
267.	William Howard Bornman	2/13/68	2/13/68
268.	John Conway Patterson	2/26/68	3/17/68
269.	Troy Denver Martin	3/8/68	3/19/68
270.	George Benjamin Williams	3/18/68	6/19/68
271.	Michael John Sanders	3/21/68	4/8/68
272.	Howard Callens Johnson	3/21/68	4/24/68
273.	George Edward Wells	3/28/68	5/27/69
274.	David Evans	4/3/68	4/26/68
275.	Franklin Allen Paris	4/9/68	5/21/68
276.	David Stuart Neff	4/18/68	4/25/68
277.	James Earl Ray	4/20/68	6/8/68
278.	John Wesley Shannon, Jr.	5/7/68	6/5/68
279.	Taylor Morris Teaford (process dismissed)	5/10/68	5/24/72
280.	Phillip Morris Jones	6/5/68	6/26/68
281.	Johnny Ray Smith	6/20/68	6/24/68
282.	Byron James Rice	7/5/68	10/2/72
283.	Robert Leroy Lindblad	7/11/68	10/7/68
284.	James Joseph Scully	7/15/68	7/23/68
285.	Billy Ray White	8/13/68	8/17/68
286.	Frederick Rudolph Yokum	8/29/68	9/6/68
287.	Harold James Evans	9/19/68	1/2/69

A CHRONOLOGICAL LISTING

	NAME	DATE ADDED	DATE APPREHENDED
288.	Robert Lee Carr	10/18/68	11/4/68
289.	Levi Washington	11/15/68	12/9/68
290.	Richard Lee Tingler	12/20/68	5/19/69
291.	George Michael Gentile	6/18/68	12/17/68
292.	Gary Steven Krist	12/20/68	12/22/68
293.	Ruth Eisemann-Schier	12/28/68	3/5/69
294.	Baltazar Garcia Estolas	1/3/69	9/3/69
295.	Billy Austin Bryant	1/8/69	1/8/69
296.	Billy Len Schales	1/27/69	1/30/69
297.	Thomas James Lucas	2/13/69	2/26/69
298.	Warren David Reddock	3/11/69	4/14/71
299.	George Edward Blue	3/20/69	3/28/69
300.	Cameron David Bishop	4/15/69	3/12/75
301.	Marie Dean Arrington	5/29/69	12/22/71
302.	Benjamin Hoskins Paddock (removed)	6/10/69	5/5/77
303.	Francis Leroy Hohimer	6/20/69	12/20/69
304.	Joseph Lloyd Thomas	9/12/69	3/8/70
305.	James John Byrnes	1/6/70	4/17/70
306.	Edmund James Devlin	3/20/70	8/15/70
307.	Lawrence Robert Plamondon	5/5/70	7/23/70
308.	Hubert Geroid Brown	5/6/70	10/16/71
309.	Angela Yvonne Davis	8/18/70	10/13/70
310.	Dwight Alan Armstrong (removed)	9/4/70	4/7/76
311.	Karleton Lewis Armstrong	9/4/70	2/16/72
312.	David Sylvan Fine	9/4/70	1/8/76
313.	Leo Frederick Burt (removed)	9/4/70	4/7/76
314.	Bernardine Rae Dohrn (process dismissed)	10/14/70	12/7/73
315.	Katherine Ann Power (removed)	10/17/70	8/15/85
316.	Susan Edith Saxe	10/17/70	3/27/75
317.	Mace Brown	10/20/72	4/18/73
318.	Herman Bell	5/9/73	9/2/73
319.	Twymon Ford Myers	9/28/73	11/14/73
320.	Ronald Harvey	12/7/73	3/27/74
321.	Samuel Richard Christian	12/7/73	12/11/73
322.	Rudolph Alonza Turner	1/10/74	10/1/74
323.	Larry Gene Cole	4/2/74	4/3/74
324.	James Ellsworth Jones	4/16/74	6/15/74
325.	Lendell Hunter	6/27/74	7/31/74
326.	John Edward Copeland, Jr.	8/15/74	7/23/75
327.	Melvin Dale Walker	10/16/74	11/9/74
328.	Thomas Otis Knight	12/12/74	12/31/74
329.	Billy Dean Anderson (killed)	1/21/75	7/7/79
330.	Robert Gerald Davis	4/4/75	8/5/77

NAME	DATE ADDED	DATE APPREHENDED
331. Richard Dean Holtan	4/18/75	7/12/75
332. Richard Bernard Lindhorst, Jr.	8/4/75	8/7/75
333. William Lewis Herron, Jr.	8/15/75	10/30/75
334. James Winston Smallwood	8/29/75	12/5/75
335. Leonard Peltier	12/22/75	2/6/76
336. Patrick James Huston	3/3/76	12/7/77
337. Thomas Edward Bethea	3/5/76	5/4/76
338. Anthony Michael Juliano	3/15/76	3/22/76
339. Joseph Maurice McDonald	4/1/76	9/15/82
340. James Ray Renton	4/7/76	5/9/77
341. Nathaniel Doyle, Jr.	4/29/76	7/15/76
342. Morris Lynn Johnson	5/25/76	6/26/76
343. Richard Joseph Picariello	7/29/76	10/21/76
344. Edward Patrick Gullion, Jr.	8/13/76	10/22/76
345. Gerhardt Julius Schwartz	11/18/76	11/22/76
346. Francis John Martin	12/17/76	2/17/77
347. Benjamin George Pavan	1/12/77	2/17/77
348. Larry Gene Campbell	3/18/77	9/6/77
349. Roy Ellsworth Smith	3/18/77	6/2/77
350. Raymond Luc Levasseur	5/5/77	11/4/84
351. James Earl Ray	6/11/77	6/13/77
352. Willie Foster Sellers	6/14/77	6/20/79
353. Larry Smith	7/15/77	8/20/77
354. Ralph Robert Cozzolino	10/19/77	1/6/78
355. Millard Oscar Hubbard	10/19/77	10/21/77
356. Carlos Alberto Torres	10/19/77	4/4/80
357. Enrique Estrada	12/5/77	12/8/77
358. William David Smith	2/10/78	10/27/78
359. Gary Ronald Warren	2/10/78	5/12/78
360. Theodore Robert Bundy	2/10/78	2/15/78
361. Andrew Evan Gipson	3/27/78	5/24/78
362. Anthony Dominic Liberatore	5/26/78	4/1/79
363. Michael George Thevis	7/10/78	11/9/78
364. Charles Everett Hughes	11/19/78	4/29/81
365. Ronald Lee Lyons	12/17/78	9/10/79
366. Leo Joseph Koury	4/20/79	Present
367. John William Sherman	8/3/79	12/17/81
368. Melvin Bay Guyon	8/9/79	8/16/79
369. George Alvin Bruton	9/28/79	12/14/79
370. Earl Edwin Austin	10/12/79	3/1/80
371. Vincent James Russo	12/24/79	1/4/81
372. Albert Victory	3/14/80	2/24/81
373. Ronald Turney Williams	4/16/80	6/8/81
374. Daniel Jay Barney (committed suicide)	3/10/81	4/19/81
375. Donald Eugene Webb	5/4/81	Present
376. Gilbert Eugene Everett	5/13/81	8/12/85
377. Leslie Nichols	7/2/81	12/17/81
378. Thomas William Manning	1/29/82	4/24/85

	NAME	DATE ADDED	DATE APPREHENDED
379.	Mutulu Shakur	7/23/82	2/11/86
380.	David Fountain Kimberly, Jr.	1/29/82	7/8/82
381.	Charles Edward Watson	10/22/82	10/25/83
382.	Laney Gibson, Jr.	11/16/83	12/18/83
383.	George Clarence Bridgette	1/13/84	1/30/84
384.	Samuel Mark Humphrey	2/29/84	3/22/84
385.	Christopher Bernard Wilder	4/5/84	8/13/84
386.	Victor Manuel Gerena	5/14/84	Present
387.	Wai-Chu Ng	6/15/84	10/4/84
388.	Alton Coleman	10/24/84	1/25/85
389.	Cleveland McKinley Davis	6/15/84	10/24/84
390.	Carmine John Persico, Jr.	1/31/85	2/15/85
391.	Lohman Ray Mays	2/15/85	9/23/85
392.	Charles Earl Hammand	3/14/85	8/4/86
393.	Michael Frederic Allen Hammand	3/14/85	8/4/86
394.	Robert Henry Nicolaus	6/28/85	7/20/85
395.	David Jay Sterling	9/30/85	2/13/86
396.	Richard Joseph Scutari	9/30/85	3/19/86
397.	Joseph William Dougherty	11/6/85	12/19/86
398.	Brian Patrick Malverty	3/28/86	4/7/86
399.	Billy Ray Waldon	5/16/86	6/16/86
400.	Claude Lafayette Dallas, Jr.	5/16/86	3/8/87
401.	Donald Keith Williams	7/18/86	8/20/86
402.	Terry Lee Connor	8/8/86	12/9/86
403.	Fillmore Raymond Cross, Jr.	8/8/86	12/23/86
404.	James Wesley Dyess	9/29/86	3/16/88
405.	Danny Michael Weeks	9/29/86	3/20/88
406.	Mike Wayne Jackson	10/1/86	10/2/86
407.	Thomas George Harrelson	11/28/86	2/9/87
408.	Robert Alan Litchfield	1/20/87	5/20/87
409.	David James Roberts	4/27/87	2/11/88
410.	Ronald Glyn Triplett	4/27/87	5/16/87
411.	Claude Daniel Marks	5/22/87	Present
412.	Donna Jean Willmott	5/22/87	Present
413.	Darren Dee O'Neall	6/25/87	2/3/88
414.	Louis Ray Beam, Jr.	7/14/87	11/6/87
415.	Ted Jeffrey Otsuki	1/22/87	9/4/88
416.	Pedro Luis Estrada	4/15/88	10/1/89
417.	John Edward Stevens	5/29/88	11/30/88
418.	Jack Darrell Farmer	5/29/88	6/1/88
419.	Roger Lee Jones	5/29/88	3/4/89
420.	Terry Lee Johnson	6/12/88	9/8/88
421.	Stanley Faison	11/27/88	12/24/88
422.	Steven Ray Stout	11/27/88	12/6/88
423.	Armando Garcia	1/8/89	Present
424.	Melvin Edward Mays	2/7/89	Present
425.	Bobby Gene Dennie	2/24/89	10/28/89
426.	Costabile "Gus" Farace	3/17/89	11/17/89

NAME	DATE ADDED	DATE APPREHENDED
427. Arthur Lee Washington, Jr.	10/18/89	Present
428. Lee Nell Carter	11/19/89	11/19/89
429. Wardell David Ford	12/20/89	Present
430. Leslie Isben Rogge	1/24/90	Present

How to Contact the FBI

Use these addresses and telephone numbers to contact the closest FBI office:

SPECIAL AGENT IN CHARGE
FEDERAL BUREAU OF INVESTIGATION
UNITED STATES DEPARTMENT OF JUSTICE

LOCATED AT:	BUILDING	TELEPHONE
ALBANY, NY 12207	502 USPO & Ct. House	518 465-7551
ALBUQUERQUE, NM 87102	301 Grand Ave., N.E.	505 247-1555
ALEXANDRIA, VA 22314	Room 500, 300 N. Lee St.	703 683-2680
ANCHORAGE, AK 99513	Fed. Bldg. Rm. E-222, 701 C St.	907 276-4441
ATLANTA, GA 30302	275 Peachtree St. N.E. 10th Fl.	404 521-3900
BALTIMORE, MD 21207	7142 Ambassador Road	301 265-8080
BIRMINGHAM, AL 35203	Room 1400, 2121 Building	205 252-7705
BOSTON, MA 02203	John F. Kennedy Federal Office Building	617 742-5533
BUFFALO, NY 14202	Room 1400-111 W. Huron St.	716 856-7800
BUTTE, MT 59702	115 US Ct House & Fed Bldg.	406 782-2304
CHARLOTTE, NC 28210	6010 Kenley Lane	704 372-5484
CHICAGO, IL 60604	Room 905, Everett McKinley Dirksen Building	312 431-1333
CINCINNATI, OH 45202	Room 9023, 550 Main Street	513 421-4310
CLEVELAND, OH 44199	3005 Federal Office Building	216 522-1400
COLUMBIA, SC 29201	1835 Assembly Street	803 254-3011
DALLAS, TX 75202	Suite 300, 1801 N. Lamar St.	214 720-2200
DENVER, CO 80202	Room 1823, Fed. Office Bldg.	303 629-7171
DETROIT, MI 48226	Patrick V. McNamara Bldg. 477 Michigan Avenue	313 965-2323
EL PASO, TX 79901	202 U.S. Court House Bldg.	915 533-7451
HONOLULU, HI 96850	Kalanianaole Federal Building Rm 4307, 300 Ala Moana Blvd.	808 521-1411
HOUSTON, TX 77002	6015 Fed. Bldg. & US CH	713 224-1511
INDIANAPOLIS, IN 46204	Rm. 679, 575 N. Penna St.	317 639-3301

LOCATED AT:	BUILDING	TELEPHONE
JACKSON, MS 39269	Federal Building, Suite 1553 100 W. Capitol Street	601 948-5000
JACKSONVILLE, FL 32211	Oaks V, 4th Floor, 7820 Arlington Expressway	904 721-1211
KANSAS CITY, MO 64106	Rm. 300 - U.S. Court House	816 221-6100
KNOXVILLE, TN 37919	Rm. 800, 1111 Northshore Dr	615 588-8571
LAS VEGAS, NV 89101	Rm. 219, Fed. Office Bldg.	702 385-1281
LITTLE ROCK, AR 72201	215 U.S. Post Office Building	501 372-7211
LOS ANGELES, CA 90024	11000 Wilshire Boulevard	213 477-6565
LOUISVILLE, KY 40202	Room 502, Federal Building	502 583-3941
MEMPHIS, TN 38103	841 Clifford Davis Federal Building	901 525-7373
MIAMI, FL 33137	3801 Biscayne Boulevard	305 573-3333
MILWAUKEE, WI 53202	Rm. 700, Federal Building and U.S. Court House	414 276-4684
MINNEAPOLIS, MN 55401	392 Federal Building	612 339-7861
MOBILE, AL 36602	One St. Louis Centre	205 438-3674
NEWARK, NJ 07102	Gateway 1, Market Street	201 622-5613
NEW HAVEN, CT 06510	Federal Bldg. 150 Court St.	203 777-6311
NEW ORLEANS, LA 70113	701 Loyola Avenue	504 522-4671
NEW YORK, NY 10278	26 Federal Plaza	212 553-2700
NORFOLK, VA 23510	Room 839, 200 Granby Mall	804 623-3111
OKLAHOMA CITY, OK 73118	50 Penn Place, Suite 1600	405 842-7471
OMAHA, NE 68102	Rm. 7401, Fed. Bldg., USPO & CH, 215 N. 17th St.	402 348-1210
PHILADELPHIA, PA 19106	8th Floor, Federal Office Bldg., 600 Arch Street	215 829-2700
PHOENIX, AZ 85012	201 E. Indianola, Suite 400	602 279-5511
PITTSBURGH, PA 15222	Rm. 1300 FOB	412 471-2000
PORTLAND, OR 97201	Crown Plaza Building	503 224-4181
RICHMOND, VA 23220	200 West Grace Street	804 644-2631
SACRAMENTO, CA 95825	Federal Building, 2800 Cottage Way	916 481-9110
ST. LOUIS, MO 63103	2704 Federal Building	314 241-5357
SALT LAKE CITY, UT 84138	3203 Federal Building	801 355-7521
SAN ANTONIO, TX 78205	Rm 433, Old PO Building, 615 E. Houston	512 225-6741
SAN DIEGO, CA 92188	Fed. Office Bldg. Rm-6S-31, 880 Front Street	619 231-1122
SAN FRANCISCO, CA 94102	450 Golden Gate Avenue	415 553-7400
SAN JUAN, PR 00918	U.S. Ct. House & Fed Bldg. Rm. 526, Hato Rey, P.R.	809 754-6000
SAVANNAH, GA 31405	5401 Paulsen Street	912 354-9911
SEATTLE, WA 98174	Rm. 710, Fed. Office Bldg. 915 Second Avenue	206 622-0460
SPRINGFIELD, IL 62702	535 W. Jefferson Street	217 522-9675
TAMPA, FL 33602	Rm. 610, Federal Office Bldg.	813 228-7661
WASHINGTON, DC 20535	FBI Washington Field Office	202 324-3000

HOW TO CONTACT THE FBI